Susan Singleton
www.singlelaw.com

About the Author

Susan Singleton is one of the UK's best known ecommerce and internet lawyers. She runs a specialist London solicitor's firm, Singletons (www.singlelaw.com), and serves clients from all over the UK and abroad. Her practice covers both internet contracts and advice on cyberlaw, as well as commercial litigation in this area. She specialises in competition/anti-trust law and intellectual property legal matters, and is author of 20 legal books and a frequent speaker at legal conferences in the UK and abroad. On the cyberlaw side, she edits *IT Law Today* and *Telecoms Law Today* journals. She has a regular consumer law slot on LBC Radio. She is married with five children.

After training at Nabarro Nathanson, she qualified as a solicitor in 1985 and moved to leading City law firm Slaughter and May where she practised competition and computer law. From there she took up a position at Bristows, a specialist London intellectual firm before founding her own firm in 1994.

LAWPACK

© 2001 Law Pack Publishing Limited

10–16 Cole Street London SE1 4YH
www.lawpack.co.uk
All rights reserved.

ISBN 1 902646 77 0

Contents

Introduction

Not since Caxton's invention of the printing press has such an important new medium of communication been introduced as email and the internet. The internet gives individuals power - power to gain access to information previously unavailable or too expensive; power to compete with bigger businesses on a level playing field; power to communicate at the click of a mouse around the world. It has largely been a power for good, but in the hands of a few can be a power for evil.

This guide aims to give you the tools to operate the internet and email lawfully. There is a common myth that the internet is unregulated; in cyberspace no one can hear you scream - or break the law. In fact, the converse applies. There are over 100 nations of the earth all with their own laws and in any internet transaction they can be fighting each other for jurisdiction. This makes legal compliance more, not less, important. Luckily, many of those laws are much the same and practical guidance can therefore be given in a guide such as this. No one should worry unduly about legal risks and the internet. The business and personal advantages to be gained far outweigh any perceived legal liabilities. Many of the risks can be minimised by appropriate notices on web sites or well-drawn-up terms and conditions for use of sites and purchase of goods or services.

There is no such thing as 'internet law' but lawyers, courts and governments have been all too quick to apply existing legislation to this field, from employment law and use of email to trade marks and domain names. Some parts of this guide will be more relevant to the reader than others. Those running a business where employees use email will find the sections about email employment policies most relevant. Those selling goods or buying goods online will want to know their rights and liabilities.

If this guide does nothing else, I hope it will alert the reader to the areas where legal advice should be sought from computer/IT lawyers. The important legal advice is often not contained in books - when to back down even when you are in the right, when is it worth spending money on a case, how much does a High Court trade mark action cost, is this matter likely to go to court. I have tried to provide answers to these practical questions, as well as describing the relevant legislation, throughout the book. Advising in the computer law field since qualification, I began working in the competition law and computer law field in 1985 in the City, at solicitors Slaughter and May, when this legal field was in its infancy. Since then I have watched it develop into an important new area which affects most people who use computers. Since founding my own London commercial law firm in 1994 I have advised on a huge range of ecommerce legal problems, from those of leading UK plcs to the dot-coms who have come and gone in the last decade. The diversity of this field, and the speed of its development, is phenomenal. It is exciting and interesting, international and important.

The law changes and in few fields as much as this. This guide is up to date to 5 September 2001. Much of the practical advice and legislation will not date quickly, but it is always wise to check by internet searches or with internet lawyers.

Any errors in the text are my own and I welcome corrections, and suggestions for amendments, as well as new instructions for legal advice at the contact details below.

I would like to thank Law Pack (particularly Jamie Ross) for their commitment to this book; my family, particularly my husband, Martin, whose sterling weekend childcare of our five children lets much of my writing be done; and my commercial clients from whose daily internet legal queries I learn at times as much as they. Finally thanks are also due to my clients Exxus Limited (www.exxus.co.uk and www.the-afs.com), Deskdemon (www.deskdemon.com), Radical Ltd (www.radicalworldwide.com) and Distinctly British Ltd (www.distinctlybritish.com), who allowed me to use some of the issues arising from their web sites by way of illustration in this book.

Susan Singleton
Pinner Hill
5 September 2001

Singletons
The Ridge
South View Road
Pinner
Middlesex HA5 3YD

Tel: 020 8866 1934
Fax: 020 8429 9212

Email: susan@singlelaw.com
Web site: www.singlelaw.com

Chapter 1

The internet and email: What's it all about?

Chapter 1

The internet and email: What's it all about?

Summary

· Uses of the internet
· Current UK/international legislation
· Policing the net
· Legal areas for businesses to watch

The internet and email have revolutionised the way businesses operate. From low-key beginnings, they have developed into an international network of computers which communicate with each other over telephone lines or microwave links. The internet is the base for the world wide web and many newsgroups. It is a means by which consumers and businesses can gain access to huge amounts of useful information across a wide range of fields. In the UK over 90 per cent of businesses and 30 per cent of households have access to the internet and use is growing quickly.

Email is the electronic transmission of letters and messages from one computer to another. Anyone with a personal computer or other internet-enabled device can send emails around the world for the price, in many cases, of a local telephone call.

This book tells you how to operate legally on the internet. It describes regulations you must follow to ensure you stay on the right side of the law, but it does not describe the technology itself. Users do not usually need to understand what is happening inside the computer or other device in order to use the technology. Nor does it tell users how to operate the internet.

The uses and abuses of the internet and email

One of the greatest uses of the internet is to obtain information quickly. Once the user has some experience of searching for information, often the internet is the easiest way of undertaking research for business or personal purposes.

Email enables people in different time zones to communicate cheaply and effectively. It allows detailed information to be sent quickly and easily, usually a lot easier than sending documents by courier.

The internet is also used for the supply of goods and services, where orders are placed online and, in the case of information or software, the 'goods' purchased are then downloaded, after payment has been made online. The purchase can be instantaneous.

The internet can also be used for unlawful or at least dubious activities. One of the biggest uses is accessing pornography, some of which is illegal in certain jurisdictions. Online betting is also a major use and increasingly the internet is being used to perpetrate frauds and scams. Get-rich-quick schemes abound to such an extent that consumer bodies such as the UK Office of Fair Trading and US Federal Trade Commission now organise internationally coordinated crackdowns.

Electronic commerce: doing business online

This book looks at legal issues arising from the internet and email, particularly those relevant to businesses. One of the greatest uses of the internet for businesses is the ability to 'do business online'. Even small companies can usually afford to set up an internet web site. This can then be accessed by anyone around the world who has an internet-enabled device.

Many company web sites do not actually offer goods or services for sale on the site; it simply acts as a glorified catalogue online ('brochureware'), telling the user where they can telephone or visit to buy the goods. Other corporate sites allow users to place an order electronically. This book provides advice in relation to both types of web sites and shows businesses the steps they need to take to protect their name and their business.

One of the most exciting and dynamic features of the Information Age is electronic commerce - conducting business and business transactions electronically. The internet is the fastest-growing market place in the world economy. Predictions are that the value of ecommerce may rise to £800 billion, or even higher, by 2003 (DTI May 2001).

Some statistics...

· One third of the UK population is now online - more than any other major European country; that is a 50 per cent increase since September 1999.

· 90 per cent of UK employees work in businesses that are connected to the internet.

· 33 per cent of people work in UK businesses that have engaged in online financial transactions with customers or suppliers.

· There has been a fourfold increase in online spending to £2 billion and the UK now has the largest ecommerce market in the EU.

· 33 per cent of UK Government services are now available online.

> ## Examples of internet uses
>
> · Advertising goods or services on a 'web site'
>
> · Searching for information about products or services
>
> · Researching technical or legal information

The law

There is no law, as such, of the internet. Instead, particular areas of existing law are applied. For example, copying someone else's business name and using it for a web site address will breach the law of trade marks. Selling goods online will involve a legal 'contract' and sale of goods legislation will apply. Sending sexually explicit emails to your secretary is just as likely to amount to sexual harassment as posting letters to them with the same content. There are few areas of law that can be avoided by using electronic rather than paper methods of communication.

Many governments around the world have, however, climbed onto the ecommerce legislative bandwagon, wanting their particular countries to be at the forefront of electronic commerce. Legislation on electronic signatures, for example, has emerged all over the world in the last few years.

The European Commission has not been slow to legislate in this area either, producing laws on electronic signatures, electronic commerce, digital copyright, distance selling to consumers and jurisdiction (i.e. where international disputes will come to court). More importantly, international legislative efforts are being made in areas as diverse as registration of internet domain names, to rounds of talks on jurisdiction and choice of law.

Policing the net

The internet is heavily policed. In the business world, it is effectively policed by both the public and private sectors.

- Large companies with well-known trade marks will have regular searches to ascertain whether their trade mark is being used by others without permission. Court proceedings will then follow in the country concerned.

- Trading standards and consumer protection bodies, both nationally and internationally, undertake regular trawls of web sites to find companies selling shoddy goods, not complying with other legislation, breaching trade descriptions or pyramid selling and the like.

· Advertising standards authorities and broadcast and other sectoral regulators monitor areas within their remit. For example, the Financial Services Authority will examine financial services web sites to ensure compliance with UK legislation.

· Police forces monitor web sites and chat rooms, even training officers to root out ageing paedophiles who lurk in chat rooms masquerading as teenagers.

· Many schools now have internet policies to be signed by pupil and parent, monitoring the use of the systems by pupils. Parents similarly can, if they choose, monitor their children's use of the internet and can purchase software which enables them to do so more easily.

· Bodies such as ICANN, the internet naming body, operate particular aspects of the internet, such as running of the domain name system.

· In some countries such as China, Vietnam and Afghanistan, there have been periods of time when only certain approved people are allowed access to the internet. In these cases, the internet has been seen as a threat as it makes it hard for states to control the information fed to its citizens.

· Bodies such as the Direct Marketing Agency (DMA) authorise use of certain symbols which indicate that a web trader is legitimate, has online terms and conditions, informs customers of extra charges and the like.

Despite the plethora of policing of what originally was set up by the academic community as an unregulated medium, free of censorship, there remain many gaps. It can be hard to trace small illegal operators who have tried to hide their location. Many web sites contain no address or contact details. Some businesses might locate their office in a country that is a tax haven or otherwise fairly unregulated. None of this should put off you off going online, either as a business or as a consumer. Those sticking to well-known reputable companies trading online will rarely have problems.

Current legislation

This book looks at relevant laws that apply when you are online. Current legislation in the UK includes:

· the Electronic Communications Act 2000;

· regulations on distance selling;

· special regulations about interception of communications (rights to read employee emails, for example);

· laws on data protection;

· the Trade Marks Act 1994, for internet domain names.

The EU has produced a large number of relevant laws that the UK Government and others have brought into force, such as a directive on electronic signatures and another on electronic commerce, one on data protection and others on copyright.

Many UK web sites are regularly viewed in the USA and it is important often to consider foreign laws too. This book gives practical guidance as to how to deal with foreign legal issues.

Main legal areas for businesses to watch

Businesses going online should consider the following:

1. Get copyright permission: Has permission been obtained for all the material to be put on the web site? Do not copy anyone else's words, pictures, sounds or other materials without their written consent, even material already on the internet on another site. Copying without permission amounts to breach of

copyright. It is sensible to put a copyright notice on the web site (e.g. '© Law Pack Publishing Limited 2001'). Chapter 2 looks at this.

2. Have written contracts with suppliers: Make sure there is a written contract with anyone other than an employee of the business, who is working on a web site or computer software for a web site. The contract will legally protect the buyer of those services and make it clear whether supplier or buyer will own copyright in the work produced and whether it can be used by the supplier on other sites or not. Contracts are dealt with in Chapter 2.

3. Comply with data protection laws: If personal data will be gathered on the site, such as customers' names and addresses when they complete forms on the site, make sure the business has notified them that it holds this data with the Information Commissioner and has paid the fees due (see www.dataprotection.gov.uk). The Data Protection Act 1998 sets out strict duties as to how such data may be used. Most web sites that gather data in this way display a privacy policy setting out how people's personal data will be used. Chapter 4 covers this.

4. Check domain names: Carry out a trade mark and Companies House search and an internet search before picking a name to be used by a business on the internet. If someone has registered as a trade mark under the Trade Marks Act 1994, then they could stop the same or a similar name being used as a domain name. Chapter 3 deals with this.

5. Have terms on the site: If goods or services are sold on the web site, then important legal information must be given to consumers under distance selling and other laws. Suppliers can also protect themselves by many of the conditions in such terms. Make sure the terms appear on the site and are clearly visible and accepted before purchase, even if no goods are sold but where the site has a lot of content.

6. Keep the site up to date: If information, product descriptions and prices on a web site are wrong, then there may be a breach of trade descriptions, advertising or other laws. Chapter 6 looks at advertising law.

7.   Have an email policy for employees: If employees will be using the email or internet at work, it is sensible to tell them what they can and cannot do with the business's systems whilst in the office. Having an email policy can make this clear and avoid misunderstandings. A sample is given in Chapter 8.

Some definitions

Email - electronic mail, a means by which two computers or other internet-enabled devices can send messages to each other.

Extranet - an extension of a intranet (defined below) to enable external users to use the system.

Internet - the international network of computer systems connected to each other.

Intranet - an internal computer network - most large UK companies run their own intranets; only those with approved access such as employees can read what information appears on the intranet.

Online - being live on a telephone line when accessing the internet or emails.

PC - personal computer.

Chapter 2

Getting your site up and running: the legal side

Chapter 2

Getting your site up and running: the legal side

Summary

· Contracts with web site designers
· Getting the rights (copyright, etc.)
· Copyright notices and intellectual property
· Terms and conditions for use of the site
· Information requirements for the web site
· Example terms and conditions
· Bulletin board rules
· Confidentiality agreements

Any business contemplating setting up a web site has two main legal areas to look at - (i) making sure its contracts with web site designers and others are properly drawn up, which is what this chapter concentrates upon, and (ii) choosing the right name or domain name for the site (which is dealt with in Chapter 3).

Before any work is done on a web site at all, legal issues should be considered. Some companies will buy ready-made web sites from companies who offer a standard service for regular monthly charges of under £100. There may be standard designs already developed and no special new contracts will be required. Companies such as www.virginbiz.com offer services such as these. The customer is unlikely, where the cost is comparatively low, to be offered much chance to negotiate the standard contract terms of the supplier. Those customers should skip the next section and go on to the 'Copyrights and intellectual property' section on p21.

However, many businesses will spend £20,000 - £100,000 or more on web site design. It is those businesses that need to make sure they have proper contracts in place, that ensure they are receiving the guarantees and warranties they need and rights to copyright and other intellectual property arising from the site design.

Tendering

For bigger web site design contracts, it is sensible to put the contract out to tender. Several suppliers may be invited to tender. For larger deals, the customer will draw up a detailed 'invitation to tender' document or 'request for information' and send it to those companies who may be suitable.

Public procurement

Any buyer in the public sector, however, needs to ensure they comply with public procurement laws. These require that high-value works, services supplies and utilities contracts must be advertised throughout the EU and very detailed legal procedures followed as to the manner in which the contract will be awarded. If the public procurement rules are not followed, then a supplier who has been excluded from the process in breach of the rules can sue for damages.

What to look for

Some companies will have their own in-house IT managers who will probably have contacts with designers and knowledge about who has offered a good service to particular sites. There may be cases where a good designer cannot be used, because, as they act for a competitor, they have a conflict of interest. On the other hand, it can be useful for more complex sites to use someone who has worked on a similar site before.

It is also wise to choose a designer who has a track record, is financially sound and is likely to be around in the years following the site's design, in case legal action against the designer for breach of contract becomes necessary. Even if such drastic action does not need to be taken, many designers are part of a company that will also host and run the site and fix bugs in it.

Make sure the designer has worked on similar sites before and has a clear idea of what needs to be done. Most disputes arise because the buyer does not communicate their requirements to the designer and had different expectations. The contract should set out these requirements in writing in detail.

Making the contract stick

Frequently large buyers of services will have standard terms and conditions they use for purchase of most services and indeed goods. They ought to have carefully thought out procedures under which the terms are sent to suppliers before any contract is made.

If the supplier replies by rejecting the buyer's terms and puts forward their own terms then that is in law a 'counter offer'. If the buyer does nothing, then the supplier's terms will apply by default. So many buyers then react by rejecting the supplier's terms, seeking to impose their own. It is important that the people at a company receiving letters or emails of this type are aware of the rules for formation of contracts, to ensure they do not accept terms that are unacceptable by default.

For bigger contracts, it is better if there is one document which is signed by both parties so there is no doubt that it is the 'entire agreement' which applies.

Buyers may have been lured into contracting with a supplier by certain promises made in sales meetings. These have a habit of fading away when it comes to writing down the contract terms and, indeed, most supplier's contracts say 'pre-contract statements do not count'. One case, Watford Electronics v Sanderson (2001), held that clauses like this do work and that two companies contracting with each other will largely be stuck with whatever the contract says. So do not assume, unless there has been a truly 'fraudulent misrepresentation', that you have the benefit of statements made by suppliers before the contract is signed.

Make the pre-contract statements include proper warranties in the agreeement so that if the supplier then breaks its promises, some money may be recoverable. IT and ecommerce solicitors are used to drafting such clauses into contracts to protect buyers.

For the large contracts, the buyer, when inviting tenders, will include its preferred contract conditions in the agreement.

Where to find contract terms

Most web site designers will have their own standard conditions of contract and many buyers use those. However, the legal position of the buyer can be significantly improved if the buyer's own contract terms are used. Contract terms can be obtained as follows:

1.   Buyers or their solicitors can write their own - IT lawyers are listed on the internet in the directory www.chambersandpartners.com and include the writer's firm, Singletons www.singlelaw.com.

2.   Some trade associations issue examples of contract terms to their members - ask yours. They cannot, however, stipulate terms that must be used, as this will breach the Competition Act 1998.

3.   Some contract term products are commercially available, such as the US Computer Law Association's CD Rom of internet/IT contracts (see www.cla.org).

4.   Some organizations, such as the Chartered Institute of Purchasing and Supply (CIPS), have model contract terms that are used in many industries and include examples of computer software contracts.

5. Some other books include contracts, such as Tolley's econtracts, which include contracts on CD Rom (£80, ISBN 0754512487, www.butterworths.com).

Always check that a contract is up to date, as the law changes on a regular basis.

Even if as a buyer you feel you want to use the supplier's terms and conditions, always read them through and do not accept they are 'set in stone'. If the supplier wants the contract they will usually be persuaded to make some changes. Make sure the changes are effected properly. They should be attached to the standard terms, or ideally be incorporated into the standard terms (which is easily done with email) and it should be made clear which prevails - the amendments or the standard terms, if there is a conflict.

Main differences between a supplier's contract and a buyer's

Supplier's	Buyer's
Will try to meet delivery date but no legal obligation.	Must stick to delivery dates or else liquidated damages to be paid.
Limited warranties about quality of the product.	Strong warranties about what the product will do, how it will look, etc.
Excludes liability very widely. In the case of breach of contract, it is the supplier's sole obligation to try to correct the problem.	Requires the supplier to put right faults/breaches of contract and entitles the buyer to damages.
Allowed to subcontract the work to someone else.	Contract must be done personally by the supplier/its direct employees.

Checklist for checking a supplier's contract

1. Does it say exactly what work will be done?

2. Does it say by which date it will be done and is there any reduction or liquidated damages paid for any delay? Is 'time of the essence' or does it say no liability for delays?

    Look out for wording such as 'reasonable endeavours' to meet the delivery date (that is a rather weak obligation which means the supplier must merely 'try' to meet the date and is very different from a clause which says the supplier will meet the date). For some buyers, time is not a problem, but for others, every week of delay amounts to lost revenue.

3. Is it clear who the supplier is? Ask for the limited company number (or full names if a sole trader) to be included. Check whether the supplier is allowed to transfer (assign) the whole contract to someone else. Must the work be done personally or could the supplier subcontract it to someone else?

4. Is there a clearly named project leader or contact person and provision for regular updates about how the work is going? Does the buyer have any input into the work as it is being done?

5. Who is responsible for ensuring copyright clearances for material to be used in designing the site? Some smaller web site designers use drawings and designs without obtaining permission from the copyright owner and the customer ends up being sued. Obtain warranties in the contract saying the designer will indemnify (pay) the customer for any losses arising from this kind of action. Also check the permissions in any event. Ask to see copies.

6. What rights are there to terminate the contract during the period when the work is being done and/or if the contract is breached.

7.   Is it a contract just for web site design or is the designer also given the right to host the site thereafter?

Getting the rights

The most common dispute with a web site designer or software supplier, after disputes over the quality of the work, is over copyright and other intellectual property rights. These are intangible rights which protect designs, drawings, computer software and trade marks and logos.

> Not surprisingly, most businesses assume if they are paying for someone to write computer software or produce drawings specifically for them, that they will automatically own the copyright in those designs. They are wrong.

The Copyright, Designs and Patents Act 1988 provides that the default position is that the author (includes designer, artist, etc.) of a copyright work keeps ownership of the copyright. All the buyer receives is a right to use the rights - a licence. This is not the same thing at all. For a start, it means that the author can licence many other companies with the same works without reference to the first customer who paid for the work. It also means that the author can sell the copyright so the licensee finds later that someone else is the licensor of the rights. It also means that if the customer wants to develop the software or works later, it needs permission from the original author, who may want an extra fee.

However, it is possible to reverse this by having an agreement in writing signed by the 'assignor' - the owner of the rights, and this is what many buyers of IT/computer software include either in their standard conditions of purchase or in a specific contract for the work.

It is not difficult or expensive for buyers to obtain copyright. A simple letter of two lines in length that makes it clear the rights will be owned by the buyer is enough.

In practice, a designer may want to use the copyright works for lots of other clients and may have two prices - one for the client to own the rights which is a high price and a cheaper price if only a simple licence is given.

Some buyers will not want ownership of the rights - just a right of use. However, such licences should be carefully drafted. The buyer may want to include a right to transfer the licence to another company in its group or to permit a third party outsourcing company to use the software - these are rights which the standard licence does not give the user, so they need to be included in the agreement in advance.

Complex copyright situations: employees and subcontractors

If a complex copyright situation arises seek legal advice. Where a copyright work is produced by an employee (but not a freelance or self-employed contractor) in the course of their employment, then the rights are automatically owned by the employer. Not all company directors are employees. Not all employees are truly 'employed' by the company - some are employees of an employment agency or work for a university or other institution or operate through their own limited company. This can cause havoc with intellectual property rights unless proper contracts are put in place.

Example

1. Mr Z designs web sites. He is very good. He offers his services through Z Designs Ltd (a company). He is not an employee of the company. He is a director and shareholder and has 25 per cent of the shares; he works for it part-time and is paid dividends on his shares. He has no contract with Z Designs.

2. Z Designs contracts with ABC Customer to design a web site. Nothing is agreed in writing about intellectual property rights.

3.   ABC is not happy with Z Designs. They want to pull out of the project and pass the work done to date to XYZ Designs who will take it over. Z Designs refuses. They say the work is their copyright.

4.   However, Mr Z did all the work. He has not agreed to transfer copyright to Z Designs. He has now fallen out with the 75 per cent shareholder of Z Designs, which has sacked him as a director. Mr Z does a deal with ABC Customer to assign them the copyright for a lump sum. Z Designs is now taking legal advice to see if Mr Z has breached his fiduciary duties as a director in taking this profit - although it was paid after he was sacked as a director.

This fictional example is typical of the real types of copyright disputes which arise in this field and which can be entirely avoided by everyone having in place written contracts dealing with ownership of rights. The cost of a copyright dispute in the High Court is rarely under £100,000 in legal fees. The cost of checking IT contracts is usually several hundred pounds. Take advice.

Copyright notices and intellectual property

Lots of information on the internet is protected by the laws of copyright. This means the words and drawings and sounds on many web pages cannot be copied without permission of the copyright owner. Just because it is in the 'public domain' does not mean it is free of copyright.

It does not matter whether there is a copyright notice on the site. The work is still protected by copyright - although such a notice is a good idea.

It does not matter whether the copyright is registered or not - in fact, in the UK copyright cannot be registered - it arises as soon as it is created.

It is irrelevant that the information has been published - it is still protected by copyright.

There is no right to copy, even if an attribution is made of the author and source. Sometimes authors allow copying on that basis, but they do not have to do so.

Copyright is not the only intellectual property right relevant to web sites. Some industrial inventions which power the internet, and computer systems, are protected by registered patent rights. In the UK, such protection is given by the Patents Act 1977. Buyers of IT/web services are unlikely to have problems with patents, however.

Trade marks are much more likely to be relevant and these are covered in the next chapter.

There is another intellectual property right called 'design' right, but it is rarely applicable and it does not protect most 'designs' on the internet (they are protected by copyright). Registered and unregistered design rights protect the aesthetic appearance of, usually, three-dimensional objects.

Although copyright will be obtained and reserved whether or not a copyright notice is put on a web site and indeed on any commercial documents, such as buyer's invitations to tender, specification documents, etc., it is sensible to 'warn off' potential infringers with such a notice and also to tell those using a site what use they can make of the copyright works on the site:

1. May they print a copy of a page of information protected by copyright?

2. May they email a copy to a friend?

3. May they save a copy to their computer's hard drive?

4. May they reproduce the information, but only for non-commercial use and only as long as it is unchanged and the author's name remains on it? (Some government web sites contain such a right.)

In practice, be aware that anything placed on a web site may be copied and the copyright owner may find it hard or expensive to prevent even clear breaches of the law, so be cautious before putting important documents on the internet.

Example copyright notice

Exxus Limited owns the web site www.exxus.co.uk and www.the-afs.com and is a site relating to sport and sports statistics.

Their copyright notice is as follows:

© Exxus Limited 2000.   All Rights Reserved.

The international symbol for copyright is ©. This should be followed by the name of the legal entity that owns the copyright. This might be a limited company, as with Exxus Ltd., or in the case of the author's solicitor's firm Singletons, it would be the name not of the firm, which is a trading name, but the sole trader - thus '© Elizabeth Susan Singleton 2001.'

With regard to the term 'All Rights Reserved', this is required in some countries to assert copyright, but this is not the case in the UK. However, it is wise to add those words.

Just about all web sites have copyright information on them. It would be hard to write a page without words appearing which comprise copyright works. Therefore it is sensible to include a copyright notice. In some countries of the world, copyright is not obtained unless a notice appears. As the web site will be seen throughout the world it is therefore an important precaution.

Confidentiality

Secret information should obviously never be put on the internet, as it will then go into the public domain and will lose

Practical tip

There is no copyright in ideas, only in their 'expression'. Anyone can 'steal' an idea. If ideas are to be protected, then confidentiality agreements must be signed before the disclosure is made. Some ideas can be protected by registered patent rights where they comprise a new industrial invention.

protection under the common law of confidence. Make sure that any ideas for web sites, business plans, etc., are marked 'confidential' and are only disclosed to web site designers, suppliers, business partners, etc., where they have signed a non-disclosure or confidentiality agreement. See example at the end of this chapter.

Terms and conditions of web site use

Do you need them?

Some web sites are little more than a glorified corporate brochure. They do not require terms and conditions for use of the site to which users must agree before using the site.

Other sites have lots of content, interactive pages - such as bulletin boards - and the sale of goods available on the site. For those types of site, it is essential to have some terms and conditions in order to protect the supplier and in some cases in order to comply with the law. At the end of this chapter is an example of terms and conditions for the use of a site (not the purchase of goods on the site) and rules of the use of a bulletin board.

At the end of Chapter 7 ('Online contracts'), an example is given of terms for the sale of goods on a site.

Terms for use of the site are recommended where:

· Articles, advice, materials, etc., appear on the site.

· There is a bulletin board on the site for users to interact with others.

· Goods and services are available for purchase on the site (in which case different conditions of sale are needed).

Separately, a privacy policy may be needed where personal data is given by users of the site. Chapter 4 considers data protection laws.

What should they say?

Like all contract terms, the terms should be clear and state a set of rules for use of the site. They are likely to cover the following areas:

· That information on the site is protected by copyright and how it may be used.

· Disclaimers - i.e. no liability for the information displayed.

· When a link can be made to the site.

· Any rules for contributions to bulletin boards - see bulletin board rules at the end of this chapter.

· When someone can be barred from the site.

When will they apply

The internet lawyer's worst nightmare, which is all-too-often realised, is when time and money are spent on drafting good terms and conditions but then the web page designers do not make them visible or accessible. If they are not drawn to the attention to the user, they may not in law apply at all. It is sensible to have them accessible through a 'terms' link on the home page and to make certain that the user clicks to signify acceptance of the terms when completing a form to register with the site.

Information requirements for a web site

All the best web sites give the full corporate name of the limited company operating the site, the registered office address and registered company number, a telephone and fax number. Those seeking to hide from customers, avoid legal liabilities and keep secret their identity reveal only an email contact address at most. This is not recommended. If goods are sold to consumers on the site, then distance selling legislation and the ecommerce directives require that such information be given, as well as information about rights to cancel the contract, returns policies, etc.

If personal data is gathered on the web site, the Data Protection Act 1998 and EU data protection directive require the identity of the data controller to be given (see Chapter 4). This information is often given in a privacy policy.

Many companies, particularly US companies, will have a corporate information web page on which they given lots of statutory details. Recent changes to English law allow UK companies to provide information to shareholders electronically, where the shareholder consents.

An example of basic corporate information on a web site is provided by Exxus:

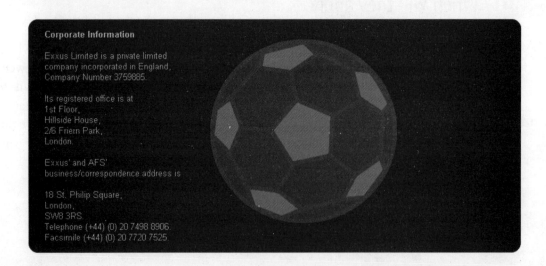

Appendix 1 to Chapter 2

Example Terms and Conditions for Use of a Web Site

Warning!

No example or precedent is appropriate for anyone. Individual legal advice should be sought and the terms should be read through entirely and will always need to be modified before use.

Web Site - Conditions of Use

1. Our terms

All use of our web site ('Site') is on these terms. If you do not agree with the terms, then cease use of the Site now. The terms are a contract between us and you may wish to print a copy for future reference. We sometimes change the terms and changes will be posted here.

2. Information

We work very hard to make sure information on the Site is accurate and up to date. Let us know if you find anything that is wrong. However, you should check independently any information before you rely on it. No representations are made by us that the information is accurate and up to date or complete and we do not accept liability for loss arising from any inaccuracy or information that is out of date. This is a web site providing information free of charge.

3. Copyright

Copyright material appears on the site which is our or our licensor's property. Do not copy anything on the Site without our prior emailed or written consent. We do not give

Web Site - Conditions of Use (continued)

permission for you to republish, alter, transmit or otherwise copy any material on the Site, but you may download information from the Site for your own personal use. Except as otherwise expressly permitted under copyright law, no copying, redistribution, retransmission, publication or commercial exploitation of downloaded material will be permitted without our express permission and that of the copyright owner.

XYZ ® is our UK registered trade mark trade mark number 12345 and all logos on this site are our trade names. You may not use them without our permission.

If you post messages on our site's bulletin board you must make sure you do not breach copyright of anyone else and if you do you must indemnify (pay) us for any loss we suffer through this. It is better to paste a link and not copy information. See also our rules for use of our bulletin board.

4.   Bulletin boards

We encourage users of the Site to contribute to our bulletin boards. See our 'Rules for Bulletin Boards' [set as hyperlink] for these terms.

5.   Liability

As information on our site is provided free of charge, we do not accept liability for it. We will not be liable to you for any indirect or consequential loss, loss of profit, revenue or good will arising from your use of the Site or information on the Site. Subject as provided below, all terms implied by law are excluded.

We accept liability for death or personal injury caused by negligence or responsibility for fraudulent misrepresentation.

6.   Supply of goods or services

Where you buy good or services from our Site you are subject to our Conditions of Supply [set as hyperlink] which supplement these conditions.

Web Site - Conditions of Use (continued)

7. Law

You agree that English law shall apply to these terms and to submit to the jurisdiction of the English courts if a dispute arises. We aim to ensure our Site complies with English law but not laws of any other country. If there is anything on the Site that you are not allowed under the laws to which you are subject to access or see, cease using the Site immediately.

8. General

Any formal legal notices should be sent to us at the address at the end of these terms by email confirmed by post.

Failure by us to enforce a right does not result in waiver of such right.

You may not assign or transfer your rights under this agreement.

We may amend these Terms at any time by posting a variation on the Site.

Further information on these terms and our contact details are here [set as hyperlink].

Appendix 2 to Chapter 2

Warning!

No example or precedent is appropriate for anyone. Individual legal advice should be sought and the terms should be read through entirely and will always need to be modified before use.

Bulletin Board Rules

These rules apply to all uses of our bulletin board. It is designed to protect us and you and to ensure everyone can use the bulletin board and benefit from it safely.

We reserve the right to remove any contributions pasted, entirely at our discretion.

We also reserve the right to disclose your personal data in response to a threat of legal action.

1. Avoid swear words and asterisks.

2. Do not libel any company or individual or let any debate become personal.

3. Pornographic and other illegal or offensive contributions are prohibited.

4. Aim to ensure debate remains relevant to the topic concerned.

5. Do not impersonate someone. Nicknames are acceptable as long as they are not offensive and are not someone else's name.

6. You may not use the bulletin board for advertising or marketing purposes whether for companies or charitable or other organisations.

7. Do not put on the Site any information which breaches copyright. If you want to refer to something appearing on the internet, then give a link and check first that the site does not prohibit links.

For further information on these rules, go to 'Corporate information' [set as hyperlink].

Appendix 3 to Chapter 2

Confidentiality Agreement

THIS AGREEMENT is made the ....200.....

BETWEEN:

(1) .... LIMITED of [*registered office address if a company*], Company No. [*No.*] (*'the Disclosing Party'*); and

(2) ('the User') of ....

WHEREAS:

(A) The User wishes to have access to certain confidential information of the Disclosing Party.

(B) The Diclosing Party is prepared to grant such access on the terms and conditions below.

1. Definition

1.1 'Confidential Information' means the information concerning the [add full description of the product/information] and other products or business of the Disclosing Party that is disclosed by the Disclosing Party to the User, whether orally, in writing or by any other means, and any other secret information concerning the business, products or customers of the Disclosing Party whether marked as confidential or not except for information in the public domain other than through the act or omission of the User.

2. Confidentiality

2.1 In consideration of being given use of the Confidential Information as set out below, the User shall, and shall procure that its employees and agents shall, keep

Confidentiality Agreement (continued)

the Confidential Information strictly confidential and not directly or indirectly reveal, report, copy, part with possession of, license, publish, transfer, communicate or disclose the Confidential Information in any manner whatsoever without the Disclosing Party's prior written consent.

2.2 The User shall ensure that the Confidential Information is stored securely and that access to it is restricted to those of its employees who need such access for the purposes of using the Confidential Information as permitted under this Agreement. The User shall ensure that it informs its employees of the specially confidential nature of the Confidential Information and shall ensure that only employees are given access to the Confidential Information. The User shall not give agents, sub-contractors, third parties or other non-employees access to the Confidential Information.

2.3 The User shall, and shall procure that its employees and agents shall, return to the Disclosing Party all the Confidential Information in material form on demand and thereupon cease to use all the Confidential Information.

2.4 The User shall indemnify the Disclosing Party from and against any loss or disclosure of the Confidential Information and all actions, proceedings, claims, demands, costs (including legal fees on a solicitor and own client basis), awards and damages however arising, directly or indirectly as a result of any breach or non-performance by the User of any of its obligations under this Agreement.

3. Permitted Purpose

3.1 The User shall only use the Confidential Information for the purpose of [evaluation of the Confidential Information - or whatever the purpose is] and not otherwise in connection with its business or other activities.

4. Intellectual Property Rights

4.1 The User shall neither acquire nor register any patents, trade marks, designs, registered designs, copyright or other intellectual property rights anywhere in the World in the Confidential Information nor acquire title to the physical materials in

Confidentiality Agreement (continued)

which the Confidential Information appears. Ownership of such rights and media shall remain with the Disclosing Party.

5. General

5.1 This Agreement is the entire agreement between the parties in connection with its subject matter and supersedes any prior agreement or other terms or representations made by the Disclosing Party to the User.

5.2 This Agreement shall continue without limit as to time.

5.3 This Agreement is subject to English law and the parties agree to submit to the jurisdiction of the English courts in relation to any dispute arising out of this Agreement.

IN WITNESS the parties have executed this Agreement as a deed on the date on page 1.

SIGNED AS A DEED
[for and on behalf of - if a company)

by   ....
            Director   Director/Company Secretary

SIGNED AS A DEED
by [.............]

in the presence of
....
Witness

[or, if a company - for and on behalf of:]
[.............]

by   ....
            Director   Director/Secretary

Chapter 3

Who owns my name?

Chapter 3

Who owns my name?

Summary

· Domain names in cyberspace
· Trade mark laws
· Avoiding infringement
· Special internet trade mark problems
· Uniform dispute resolution procedure
· Resolving disputes
· Sample trade mark notice

Just as post codes are used for particular street names, computers connected to the internet have unique numerical addresses so that electronic information is delivered to the right place. The Domain Name System (DNS) translates the numerical addresses of computers into more user-friendly names. The resulting domain names are easy to recall and help people to find information on the internet.

Nominet, UK registry for domain names

The ability for human beings to name themselves and to differentiate themselves from others is fundamental to the human condition. Virtually every society, primitive or otherwise, has names and it is not surprising that names in cyberspace are as important as in any other context. When big business becomes involved - and a lot of money is at stake - the sparks fly and the lawyers come out in force.

Domain names in cyberspace

Anyone starting to operate on the internet for the first time should check the name they want to use at a very early stage, and certainly before any money is spent.

Most readers will be familiar with web site addresses such as the writer's www.singlelaw.com. These are known as URLs (uniform resource locators). Domain names are used in an email address - the writer's is susan@singlelaw.com. People use that address as the one to which to send emails.

The existing top level domains (TLDs) - the part that comes at the end of the name, the 'suffix' - are well known: '.co.uk' and '.com', also '.net', '.org', etc.

Seven new TLDs have also been announced:

TLD	Purpose	Applicant
.aero	Air-transport industry	Societe Internationale de Telecommunications Aeronautiques SC (SITA)
.biz	Businesses	JVTeam, LLC (now known as NeuLevel) - available 1 October 2001 but earlier for existing domain owners
.coop	Non-profit cooperatives	National Cooperative Business Association (NCBA)
.info	Unrestricted use	Afilias, LLC (due to start 19 September 2001)
.museum	Museums	Museum Domain Management Association (MDMA)
.name	For registration by individuals	Global Name Registry Ltd
.pro	Accountants, lawyers, and physicians	RegistryPro Ltd

For further information on the history of ICANN's TLD application process, see www.icann.org/tlds/.

There is no need to register every combination of a name, although bigger companies will find it best to do so where money is no object.

Trade mark laws

The most important issue is registered trade marks. These usually prevail over a registered domain name or even a limited company name registered in the UK at Companies House.

Action before using a new domain name

1. Do a search at the UK trade marks registry for the name concerned and for similar names. Either use a trade mark agent who is a member of ITMA, the Institute of Trade Mark Attorneys (www.itma.org.uk) or contact the UK trade mark agent direct (see www.patent.gov.uk/tm/index.htm).

2. Do a search at Companies House (www.companieshouse.gov.uk). It is free of charge to search online the names of the same or similar sounding corporate names.

3. Not all businesses will have registered trade marks or indeed their corporate names registered, as some are sole traders who do not need to register, and many use names other than their business name for their products and services, so look in trade journals, do internet searches on any search engine and generally look out for companies with similar sounding names.

Avoiding infringement

Avoid trouble early and before money is spent.

· A typical High Court trade mark action will result in legal costs of £100,000 - £200,000.

· A typical solicitor's letter warning off a trade mark infringer is likely to cost about £300 to put together.

· Some businesses spend over £100,000, and some millions, on a branding exercise. Checking who else may own the same name in advance can save a fortune.

So what does registered trade mark law say? First, if someone has registered a UK trade mark, no-one else is allowed in the UK to use the same or a confusingly similar name for the same class of goods or services for which the mark was registered. Foreign trade marks have similar rights. Sometimes use of the mark in a very different field can also be prevented, if there is sufficient goodwill and reputation in the trade mark.

Never pick a trade mark that is too like another. The best names are entirely new, invented words. Picking a name that is generic is likely to mean it could never be registered as a trade mark in any event.

Make sure the name is not a rude word in another language in a country which is an important market for the company.

Also, if choosing a new name, do consider registering it as a registered trade mark in all major markets to preserve the trade mark rights in the name. Registering as a domain name does not secure registered trade mark protection.

If protection is required in more than two or three EU states, then it is cheaper to apply for a Community Trade Mark, which is one trade mark across the whole of the

EU, rather than paying to register in each individual EU state where protection is needed. A trade mark agent is the best person to advise on where to register abroad.

Special internet trade mark problems

Web sites can be viewed around the world. It is not uncommon for two companies in different countries to have the same name. That is not a problem when each serves customers in their own country only and each may even have their own registered trade mark there. It does become a problem when they go online, as any customer doing an internet search may find the rival from the other country. What should the companies do?

- Often the bigger company will send lawyers' letters to the smaller and bully them into giving up the name.

- The company with the registered trade mark will usually win any domain name dispute.

- Sometimes each party with a similar name can provide a link on their web site to the site of the other, so that if people reach one site by mistake then they can be referred to the other site. Trade mark lawyers often draw up contracts between two warring parties setting out how each will use a similar name.

- Each could adopt a domain that makes it clear what goods they sell through the name itself. Adding an extra word, such as 'lawpackbooks.com', could do this.

- One could buy the name of the other.

If one company is using the same name, but for different products, there may be no confusion in ordinary business, but when web sites and the internet become involved, a customer doing a search will not search by class of products so the two will suddenly find confusion. Two companies called Prince ended up fighting each other in court, in one case.

Jurisdiction issues become important. Cases in the US and UK and elsewhere have often looked at when a web site is directed at customers abroad and when it does not. There will only be breach of trade mark rights where the site is targeting or marketing to customers in the country where the other party has its reputation and/or trade mark. Jurisdiction is dealt with in Chapter 5.

Case examples

1. Crate & Barrell: Euromarket v Peters

In the case of Euromarket Designs Inc. v Peters (25 July 2001) the English court held that using the trade mark 'crate and barrel' on a web site operated by a retail outlet in the Irish Republic did not necessarily breach a trade mark of a well-known US chain of furniture stores (called Crate & Barrel) in the UK. The US company owned a UK trade mark and wanted to stop the small Dublin shop advertising through its web site. The use of a mark must be 'in the course of trade in relation to goods and services in the European Member State concerned', the judge held. The Dublin shop was not using the trade mark in the UK, even though people could access the Dublin web site from the UK and even though prices were shown in US dollars and a .com name was used. There had been no orders from the UK.

2. Roadrunner: Road Tech Computer Systems Ltd v Mandata (Management and Data Services Ltd) (25 May 2000) - Metatags

Here the English courts examined 'metatags', devices hidden on a site which embed a competitor's trade mark on the other party's web site without their permission to divert people searching for the other site and win business that way. The parties supplied software to the road haulage industry. The trade marks were 'Roadrunner' and 'Road Tech'. The defendant had used them in its metatags and as a hidden text on the first page of the site. The claimant sued for trade mark infringement and passing off. They obtained a summary judgment, which is where a court decides a case early on, on an early application by one party where there is no good defence, normally after a few months rather than the period of years a case often takes to reach a full trial. The defendant had been falsely indicating to internet users that the defendant's site was connected to the claimant's.

3. 1-800 Flowers Inc. v Phonenames Ltd. (17 May 2001)

In this case a US florist '1-800 Flowers' was sued. It owned a trade mark for '800-FLOWERS'. When this was dialled numerically it was a trade mark owned by the UK company, Phonenames. The US company said that although it did not actively market its services in the UK, UK customers could access it by telephone or online on a US web site. The court said there was no evidence to illustrate that there had been an attempt to attract business from the UK. There had been no orders made by customers from the UK by telephone or online and the appeal was rejected.

Unregistered trade marks

Even if no application has been made for a registered trade mark, English law and the laws of some other states protect unregistered trade marks on which goodwill has been built up through laws known as 'passing off'. This can be harder to prove than trade mark infringement, as there is no certificate of ownership, but in particular, if confusion can be shown, then someone using the name without permission may be sued. Take legal advice.

Examples

1. Sometimes, a descriptive name is sensible for commercial reasons. One of the author's clients is Distinctly British Ltd. Their web site sells British goods and they chose www.distinctlybritish.com as their domain name. Their logo below also appears on their web site:

distinctlybritish.com
Quality Goods in the British Tradition

2. Another client example is Desk Demon. Their site provides information and services to office workers and the name is in part descriptive of the services provided:

3. A third is Radical Limited, which provides global logistics modelling software and services. Their domain name is www.radicalworldwide.com.

    Their logo is displayed on the web site on each page.

Trade names: '.Radical' and the Radical logo are the property of Radical.

Their legal notices section informs users of the site that the company is claiming rights in the trade names used.

Legal notices

As can be seen from the examples above, companies need to consider not only registering their name on the internet as a domain name, but also contacting the UK Trade Marks Registry (www.patent.gov.uk) to register a registered trade mark. Some companies have lots of different trade marks which may not be the same as their domain name. A food manufacturer for example might have 100 food brand names but one company name. It would register the company name in most cases as its domain name but where on the web site it refers to products which are protected by trade marks it would indicate, as it would do in its printed marketing material, which names are registered trade marks. A look at any large company's web site will show how this is done.

ICANN

The international body in charge of domain names is ICANN, the Internet Corporation for Assigned Names and Numbers (www.icann.org), which is one of the best sources of information in this area. It describes itself as a 'non-profit corporation that was formed to assume responsibility for the IP address space allocation, protocol parameter assignment, domain name system management, and root server system management functions previously performed under U.S. Government contract by IANA and other entities'.

Uniform Dispute Resolution Procedure

Some domain name disputes can be handled cheaply through the Uniform Dispute Resolution Procedure (UDRP) operated by ICANN and the World Intellectual Property Organisation (WIPO, www.wipo.org). All registrars in the .com, .net, and .org top-level domains follow the UDRP.

Those in the UK with .co.uk, however, need to follow a slightly different resolution procedure - if they choose to do so rather than going to court - operated by Nominet. At the date of writing, its terms were under review.

Cybersquatters

Giving in to cybersquatters (those hijacking your name and holding it to ransom) sets a bad precedent. If costs are an issue, try the resolution procedures operated by

Nominet (www.nominet.org.uk, for .co.uk domains) and ICANN or WIPO (www.icann.org and www.wipo.org) for others. They do not lead to awards of damages or legal costs, but they can result in the name being handed over to the true owner, which may be the simple remedy the complainant wants. The US has specific cybersquatting legislation that sets out when use of someone else's name is bona fide.

Difficulties occur when a name is used to denigrate its true owner - sometimes a fan club is set up without approval by a famous person and there are many dot.sucks sites on the internet. In slang terms, when someone derogates another person or company, they often say they 'suck' in the US and in internet slang and increasingly English slang too. Thus downingstreetsucks.com could be a web site devoted to criticism of the Government. There are thousands of sites on the internet with '.sucks' in their name designed for this purpose.

Resolving disputes

1. Make sure disputes do not arise, by picking a name which is not in use in the first place.

2. Settle disputes early before lots of money is spent on legal fees and lots of management time wasted. Never litigate on principle.

3. For valuable trade marks, litigation may become necessary. In the English case One in a Million, some well-known English companies, which owned trade marks for their names, sued an internet cybersquatter who had registered their names simply in order to 'cash in' by selling those names back to their rightful trade mark owners. The court said the names should be handed back to Marks & Spencer, Virgin and the other companies for nothing. Do not let breaches continue or rights can be lost.

4. Do a cost analysis to determine the best means of settling the dispute.

Appendix

Sample registered trade mark notice:

'ABC ® is a registered trade mark of ABC Limited. All rights reserved.'

Sample unregistered trade name notice:

'ABC ™ is a trade name of ABC Limited. All rights reserved'.

This latter example is for names that are not registered at the Trade Marks Registry, but which qualify for protection by the passing off law.

Chapter 4

Data protection, email and spamming

Chapter 4

Data protection, email and spamming

Summary
· Spam
· Unsolicited emails - what the law allows
· Privacy policies for web sites
· Export of personal data
· Email preference schemes
· EU standard clauses for export of data
· Example privacy policy

Ten years ago, few UK businesses used email. Now for many companies 90 per cent or more of their business correspondence is by email. It has proved a cheap, effective and efficient method of communication. Although there are scare stories about hackers and worries about viruses, in most cases, email operates very well with few problems. Letters posted go astray. Even documents sent by courier can be lost. Email is not necessarily any more likely to result in the message not reaching the recipient.

This chapter looks at data protection legislation and in particular 'spam' - the sending of emails for marketing purposes. At the end of the chapter is an example of a privacy policy for a web site. The use and abuse of email and the internet by employees, employment email policies and issues relating to surveillance of employee emails are dealt with in Chapter 8. What information should appear at the foot or head of an email is also considered there. Computer viruses are examined in Chapter 9.

Spam

Unsolicited email is sometimes called 'spam'. Many readers will already be aware of the amount of 'junk mail' sent by email, which abounds, and many will regret ever having registered at web sites, the operators of which then begin to bombard them with unwanted messages. Although there have been obscure legal cases over the years about whether sending an unsolicited fax amounts to theft of the recipient's paper, in general the law allows anyone to communicate with anyone else. Thus, a citizen can, if they choose, write to the Prime Minister. There is no obligation on the recipient to read the communication but usually no offence is committed. This is the legal starting point.

How the law may interfere is if the details being used are what is called 'personal data'. This is defined in the Data Protection Act 1998 and, indeed, in the EU data protection directive on which it is based. It includes personal details about a living individual. Thus 'Managing Director, XYZ Ltd' is not personal data but 'Mr. John Smith, XYZ Ltd' is. The Government has an 'Information Commissioner' who is responsible for this area - formally called the Data Protection Commissioner or Registrar. The current incumbent is Mrs Elizabeth France (web site www.dataprotection.gov.uk). Email addresses are classed as personal data and so is most of the information individuals can be asked to complete on registration forms on web sites.

Some sites require people to register before they can use the site. However, that often discourages people from using the site, so is not usually a good commercial requirement when the aim is to have as many people as possible using the site and returning regularly because they like it and when it is updated on a regular basis.

Others require users to register in order to be sent information about development or products. Those users are then volunteering their personal data and often expressly agreeing to follow-up emails. The better sites let them 'unsubscribe' quite easily to such mailings later and set out a simple procedure to do this.

Unsolicited emails – what the law allows

The Data Protection Act 1998 is a complicated statute. There is some guidance on the Commissioner's web site about the use of the internet for 'data controllers' (people controlling personal data) and 'data subjects' (people whose data is being used). Those guidelines emphasise the requirements of the 1998 Act. The Act sets out eight principles of data protection that all those controlling personal data must follow, such as keeping the data safe and secure and up to date and, most importantly of all, only using it for the purposes for which it was obtained and ceasing to process it if the individual objects later.

Opting in or out?

At the date of writing, the European Commission is considering some new laws (see 'Further information') which might require that unsolicited emails (spam) may only be sent if the individual has specifically consented (i.e. clicked a box to indicate expressly that they would like commercial communications or spam to be sent to them), rather than permitting this unless the individual objects. Some countries in the EU already have such opt-in rules and others remain with opting out. It is an important issue, because in practice individuals often do nothing - so if that automatically opts them in, the data controller thus gains rights to use a lot of valuable data. If the default position instead is that no such use of their data can be made, then the data controller loses the right to process it in this way.

It is not entirely clear what the 1998 Act currently provides in this area. It says individuals must give consent to the processing of their data and the direct mail industry and Information Commissioner take opposing views. A legal challenge is likely, but meanwhile, to be on the safe side, many companies have moved to opting in, from the previous opting out procedure, but by no means all companies have taken such a cautious attitude.

Where sensitive personal data is involved, such as information about race, religion, sex, etc., then the individual must give 'specific' consent to the processing of the data.

Privacy policies for web sites

Many web sites have a written policy about data protection. There is no legal requirement to have one, but there is a legal requirement under the 1998 Act to notify data subjects of certain information, such as the full name of the company that is the data controller and the purposes for which the data is gathered. It is therefore a good idea to put it into a privacy policy. An example of one is at the end of this chapter, but they vary substantially depending on to which uses the data will be put.

Data symbol

The Information Commissioner has issued a logo that businesses can use when they gather data:

The signpost has been devised for use by organisations requesting personal information and must only be used in conjunction with an explanation of why the information is being requested and for what purpose(s) it will be used.

Source: Information Commissioner's web site
www.dataprotection.gov.uk

Practical advice

When signing up users on a web site, offer the following:

1. A right to opt in to receiving further information about products and services.

2. An easy means to unsubscribe later.

3. A clear privacy policy setting out how their data will be used.

4. Clear details of what personal data of theirs will be held or used and by whom.

Notifying the holding of data

The Data Protection Act 1998 also requires that all those holding personal data must notify the Information Commissioner (register). This costs £35 a year. Most businesses in the UK should be registered. A company can check whether it or someone else is registered, free of charge, by searching at www.dpr.gov.uk.

Subject access

The Act gives individuals a right to demand to see copies of the personal data that are held about them. Many people checking their credit history will make such requests. The Information Commissioner has set out useful guidance on how this right applies where the personal data is contained in emails held by the company concerned. In extreme cases, it may even be necessary to recover the information in deleted emails (which is often technically possible despite the deletion) in order to comply with such a 'subject access' request.

Exporting data

Companies that gather data abroad and process it there and are not connected with the EU should consider their own and usually not EU/UK data protection laws. However, UK companies exporting data from the UK/EU to countries that do not have the same strong data protection legislation must consider the impact of the legislation. A lot of data is shipped abroad where labour costs are lower, so it can be processed more cheaply.

The eighth data protection principle provides that personal data must not be shipped outside the EU/EEA without consent of the individual or where other conditions are satisfied to countries without adequate data protection legislation. Switzerland and Hungary have been found to have adequate laws and there is a special Safe Harbor Agreement with the US, whereby companies who register under it may then export data freely between the US and EEA (although few US companies have signed that agreement). Export is permitted in certain cases, so it is always worth taking legal advice.

In June 2001, the European Commission agreed a set of standard clauses that can be used where data is to be exported. Where the recipient of the data signs the clauses, the export may go ahead. The clauses are reproduced at the end of this chapter.

Email preference schemes

There is a voluntary email preference scheme that companies can join if they wish and which gives individuals the right to opt out of unsolicited emails. However, it currently only applies to those companies who join the scheme. Much of the spam which afflicts email users will come from sites that are not members of any such scheme. If the EU legislation which may require opting in, not opting out, for email goes through then this scheme may be extended along the lines of the current Fax Preference Service. EU laws prohibit absolutely the sending of unsolicited faxes to individuals (and also to companies where the company has registered with the FPS).

Breaching the law

A breach of the Data Protection Act 1998 can lead to a fine of up to £5,000, so companies should do their best to be compliant. In any event, consumers are put off using web sites that do not conform to the standard, good, privacy practices of the better web sites. Looking at any large consumer-orientated web site will show the types of data protection issues which are addressed by such bigger companies. Smaller businesses would be well advised to follow suit.

Appendix 1 to Chapter 4

Model Clauses for Export of Data from the EU Approved June 2001

Standard contractual clauses
for the purposes of Article 26(2) of Directive 95/46/EC for the transfer of personal data to third
countries which do not ensure an adequate level of protection

Name of the data exporting organisation:..
Address:..

....

Tel.:.....................; *Fax:*......................; *Email:*......................................

Other information needed to identify the organisation:..

....
                                                                            ('the Data Exporter')
and
Name of the data importing organisation:...
Address:..

....

Tel:.....................; *Fax:*......................; *Email:*......................................

Other information needed to identify the organisation:..
                                                                            ('the Data Importer')

HAVE AGREED on the following contractual clauses ('the **Clauses**') in order to adduce
adequate safeguards with respect to the protection of privacy and fundamental rights and
freedoms of individuals for the transfer by the Data Exporter to the Data Importer of
the personal data specified in Appendix 1.

Model Clauses for Export of Data from the EU Approved June 2001 (continued)

Clause 1
Definitions

For the purposes of the Clauses:

(a)   'personal data', 'special categories of data', 'process/processing', 'controller', 'processor', 'Data Subject' and 'Supervisory Authority' shall have the same meaning as in Directive 95/46/EC of 24 October 1995 on the protection of individuals with regard to the processing of personal data and on the free movement of such data ('the Directive');

(b)   'the Data Exporter' shall mean the Controller who transfers the Personal Data;

(c)   'the Data Importer' shall mean the Controller who agrees to receive from the Data Exporter personal data for further processing in accordance with the terms of these Clauses and who is not subject to a third country's system ensuring adequate protection.

Clause 2
Details of the Transfer

The details of the transfer, and in particular the categories of personal data and the purposes for which they are transferred, are specified in Appendix 1 which forms an integral part of the Clauses.

Clause 3
Third-party beneficiary clause

The Data Subjects can enforce this Clause, Clause 4 (b), (c) and (d), Clause 5 (a), (b), (c) and (e), Clause 6 (1) and (2), and Clauses 7, 9 and 11 as third-party beneficiaries. The parties do not object to the Data Subjects being represented by an association or other bodies if they so wish and if permitted by national law.

Model Clauses for Export of Data from the EU Approved June 2001 (continued)

Clause 4
Obligations of the Data Exporter

The Data Exporter agrees and warrants:

(a)   that the processing, including the transfer itself, of the personal data by him has been and, up to the moment of the transfer, will continue to be, carried out in accordance with all the relevant provisions of the Member State in which the Data Exporter is established (and where applicable has been notified to the relevant Authorities of that State) and does not violate the relevant provisions of that State;

(b)   that if the transfer involves special categories of Data the Data Subject has been informed or will be informed before the transfer that his data could be transmitted to a third country not providing adequate protection;

(c)   to make available to the Data Subjects upon request a copy of the Clauses; and

(d)   to respond in a reasonable time and to the extent reasonably possible to enquiries from the Supervisory Authority on the processing of the relevant Personal Data by the Data Importer and to any enquiries from the Data Subject concerning the processing of his Personal Data by the Data Importer.

Clause 5
Obligations of the Data Importer

The Data Importer agrees and warrants:

(a)   that he has no reason to believe that the legislation applicable to him prevents him from fulfilling his obligations under the contract and that in the event of a change in that legislation which is likely to have a substantial adverse effect on the guarantees provided by the Clauses, he will notify the change to the Data Exporter and to the Supervisory Authority where the Data Exporter is established, in which case the Data Exporter is entitled to suspend the transfer

---

Model Clauses for Export of Data from the EU Approved June 2001 (continued)

of data and/or terminate the contract;

(b) to process the Personal Data in accordance with the Mandatory Data Protection Principles set out in Appendix 2;

or, if explicitly agreed by the parties by ticking below and subject to compliance with the Mandatory Data Protection Principles set out in Appendix 3, to process in all other respects the data in accordance with:

- the relevant provisions of national law (attached to these Clauses) protecting the fundamental rights and freedoms of natural persons, and in particular their right to privacy with respect to the processing of personal data applicable to a Data Controller in the country in which the Data Exporter is established, or,

- the relevant provisions of any Commission decision under Article 25(6) of Directive 95/46/EC finding that a third country provides adequate protection in certain sectors of activity only, if the Data Importer is based in that third country and is not covered by those provisions, in- so-far as those provisions are of a nature which makes them applicable in the sector of the transfer;

(c) to deal promptly and properly with all reasonable inquiries from the Data Exporter or the Data Subject relating to his processing of the Personal Data subject to the transfer and to cooperate with the competent Supervisory Authority in the course of all its enquiries and abide by the advice of the Supervisory Authority with regard to the processing of the data transferred;

(d) at the request of the Data Exporter to submit its data processing facilities for audit which shall be carried out by the Data Exporter or an inspection body composed of independent members and in possession of the required professional qualifications, selected by the Data Exporter, where applicable, in agreement with the Supervisory Authority;

Model Clauses for Export of Data from the EU Approved June 2001 (continued)

(e)   to make available to the Data Subject upon request a copy of the Clauses and indicate the office which handles complaints.

Clause 6
Liability

1.   The Parties agree that a Data Subject who has suffered damage as a result of any violation of the provisions referred to in Clause 3 is entitled to receive compensation from the parties for the damage suffered. The Parties agree that they may be exempted from this liability only if they prove that neither of them is responsible for the violation of those provisions.

2.   The Data Exporter and the Data Importer agree that they will be jointly and severally liable for damage to the Data Subject resulting from any violation referred to in paragraph 1. In the event of such a violation, the Data Subject may bring an action before a court against either the Data Exporter or the Data Importer or both.

3.   The parties agree that if one party is held liable for a violation referred to in paragraph 1 by the other party, the latter will, to the extent to which it is liable, indemnify the first party for any cost, charge, damages, expenses or loss it has incurred.*

[paragraph 3 is optional]*

Clause 7
Mediation and Jurisdiction

1.   The parties agree that if there is a dispute between a Data Subject and either party which is not amicably resolved and the Data Subject invokes the third-party beneficiary provision in Clause 3, they accept the decision of the Data Subject:

(a)   to refer the dispute to mediation by an independent person or, where applicable, by the Supervisory Authority;

Model Clauses for Export of Data from the EU Approved June 2001 (continued)

(b)   to refer the dispute to the courts in the Member State in which the Data Exporter is established.

2.   The Parties agree that by agreement between a Data Subject and the relevant party a dispute can be referred to an arbitration body, if that party is established in a country that has ratified the New York Convention on enforcement of arbitration awards.

3.   The parties agree that paragraphs 1 and 2 apply without prejudice to the Data Subject's substantive or procedural rights to seek remedies in accordance with other provisions of national or international law.

Clause 8
Cooperation with Supervisory Authorities

The parties agree to deposit a copy of this contract with the Supervisory Authority if it so requests or if such deposit is required under national law.

Clause 9
Termination of the Clauses

The parties agree that the termination of the Clauses at any time, in any circumstances and for whatever reason does not exempt them from the obligations and/or conditions under the Clauses as regards the processing of the data transferred.

Clause 10
Governing Law

The Clauses shall be governed by the law of the Member State in which the Data Exporter is established, namely ....

Model Clauses for Export of Data from the EU Approved June 2001 (continued)

Clause 11
Variation of the contract

The parties undertake not to vary or modify the terms of the Clauses.

On behalf of the Data Exporter:

Name *(written out in full)*:...

Position:...

Address:...

Other information necessary in order for the contract to be binding *(if any)*:

....

Signature:...

(stamp of organisation)

On behalf of the Data Importer:

Name *(written out in full)*:...

Position:...

Address:...

Other information necessary in order for the contract to be binding *(if any)*:

....

Signature...

(stamp of organisation)

APPENDIX 1 to the Standard Contractual Clauses

This Appendix forms part of the Clauses and must be completed and signed by the parties (*The Member States may complete or specify, according to their national procedures, any additional necessary information to be contained in this Appendix)

Model Clauses for Export of Data from the EU Approved June 2001 (continued)

Data Exporter

The Data Exporter is *(please specify briefly your activities relevant to the transfer)*:

....

....

Data Importer

The Data Importer is *(please specify briefly your activities relevant to the transfer)*:

....

....

Data Subjects

The personal data transferred concern the following categories of Data Subjects *(please specify)*:

....

....

Purposes of the transfer

The transfer is necessary for the following purposes *(please specify)*:

....

....

Categories of data

The personal data transferred fall within the following categories of data *(please specify)*:

....

....

Sensitive Data (if appropriate)

The personal data transferred fall within the following categories of sensitive data *(please specify)*:

....

....

Model Clauses for Export of Data from the EU Approved June 2001 (continued)

Recipients

The personal data transferred may be disclosed only to the following recipients or categories of recipients *(please specify):*

....

....

Storage limit

The personal data transferred may be stored for no more than *(please indicate):* ....*(months/years):*

	DATA EXPORTER	DATA IMPORTER
Name:	....	....
Authorised Signature:	....	....

APPENDIX 2 to the Standard Contractual Clauses

Mandatory Data Protection Principles referred to in the first paragraph of Clause 5(b). These data protection principles should be read and interpreted in the light of the provisions (principles and relevant exceptions) of Directive 95/46/EC.

They shall apply subject to the mandatory requirements of the national legislation applicable to the Data Importer which do not go beyond what is necessary in a democratic society on the basis of one of the interests listed in Article 13(1) of Directive 95/46/EC, that is, if they constitute a necessary measure to safeguard national security, defence, public security, the prevention, investigation, detection and prosecution of criminal offences or of breaches of ethics for the regulated professions, an important economic or financial interest of the State or the protection of the Data Subject or the rights and freedoms of others.

Model Clauses for Export of Data from the EU Approved June 2001 (continued)

(1) **Purpose limitation**

Data must be processed and subsequently used or further communicated only for the specific purposes in Appendix 1 to the Clauses. Data must not be kept longer than necessary for the purposes for which they are transferred.

(2) **Data quality and proportionality**

Data must be accurate and, where necessary, kept up to date. The data must be adequate, relevant and not excessive in relation to the purposes for which they are transferred and further processed.

(3) **Transparency**

Data Subjects must be provided with information as to the purposes of the processing and the identity of the data controller in the third country, and other information insofar as this is necessary to ensure fair processing, unless such information has already been given by the Data Exporter.

(4) **Security and confidentiality**

Technical and organisational security measures must be taken by the data controller that are appropriate to the risks, such as unauthorised access, presented by the processing. Any person acting under the authority of the data controller, including a processor, must not process the data except on instructions from the controller.

(5) **Rights of access, rectification, erasure and blocking of data**

As provided for in Article 12 of Directive 95/46/EC, the Data Subject must have a right of access to all data relating to him that are processed and, as appropriate, the right to the rectification, erasure or blocking of data, the processing of which does not comply with the principles set out in this Appendix, in particular because the data are incomplete or inaccurate. He should also be able to object to the processing of the data relating to him on compelling legitimate grounds relating to his particular situation.

(6) **Restrictions on onward transfers**

Further transfers of personal data from the Data Importer to another controller

Model Clauses for Export of Data from the EU Approved June 2001 (continued)

established in a third country not providing adequate protection or not covered by a Decision adopted by the Commission pursuant to Article 25(6) of Directive 95/46/EC (onward transfer) may take place only if either:

(a) Data Subjects have, in the case of special categories of data, given their unambiguous consent to the onward transfer or, in other cases, have been given the opportunity to object.

The minimum information to be provided to Data Subjects must contain in a language understandable to them:
- the purposes of the onward transfer,
- the identification of the Data Exporter established in the Community,
- the categories of further recipients of the data and the countries of destination, and
- an explanation that, after the onward transfer, the data may be processed by a controller established in a country where there is not an adequate level of protection of the privacy of individuals; or

(b) the Data Exporter and the Data Importer agree to the adherence to the Clauses of another controller which thereby becomes a party to the Clauses and assumes the same obligations as the Data Importer.

(7) **Special categories of data**

Where data revealing racial or ethnic origin, political opinions, religious or philosophical beliefs or trade union memberships and data concerning health or sex life and data relating to offences, criminal convictions or security measures are processed, additional safeguards should be in place within the meaning of Directive 95/46/EC, in particular, appropriate security measures such as strong encryption for transmission or such as keeping a record of access to sensitive data.

(8) **Direct marketing**

Where data are processed for the purposes of direct marketing, effective procedures

Model Clauses for Export of Data from the EU Approved June 2001 (continued)

should exist allowing the Data Subject at any time to 'opt out' from having his data used for such purposes.

(9) **Automated individual decisions**

Data Subjects are entitled not to be subject to a decision which is based solely on automated processing of data, unless other measures are taken to safeguard the individual's legitimate interests as provided for in Article 15(2) of Directive 95/46/EC. Where the purpose of the transfer is the taking of an automated decision as referred to in Article 15 of Directive 95/46/EC, which produces legal effects concerning the individual or significantly affects him and which is based solely on automated processing of data intended to evaluate certain personal aspects relating to him, such as his performance at work, creditworthiness, reliability, conduct, etc., the individual should have the right to know the reasoning for this Decision.

APPENDIX 3 to the Standard Contractual Clauses

Mandatory Data Protection Principles referred to in the second paragraph of Clause 5(b).

(1) **Purpose limitation**

Data must be processed and subsequently used or further communicated only for the specific purposes in Appendix 1 to the Clauses. Data must not be kept longer than necessary for the purposes for which they are transferred.

(2) **Rights of access, rectification, erasure and blocking of data**

As provided for in Article 12 of Directive 95/46/EC, the Data Subject must have a right of access to all data relating to him that are processed and, as appropriate, the right to the rectification, erasure or blocking of data the processing of which does not comply with the principles set out in this Appendix, in particular because the data is incomplete or inaccurate. He should also be able to object to

Model Clauses for Export of Data from the EU Approved June 2001 (continued)

the processing of the data relating to him on compelling legitimate grounds relating to his particular situation.

(3) **Restrictions on onward transfers**

Further transfers of personal data from the Data Importer to another controller established in a third country not providing adequate protection or not covered by a Decision adopted by the Commission pursuant to Article 25(6) of Directive 95/46/EC (onward transfer) may take place only if either:

(a) Data Subjects have, in the case of if special categories of data, given their unambiguous consent to the onward transfer, or, in other cases, have been given the opportunity to object.

The minimum information to be provided to Data Subjects must contain in a language understandable to them:

- the purposes of the onward transfer,
- the identification of the Data Exporter established in the Community,
- the categories of further recipients of the data and the countries of destination, and,
- an explanation that, after the onward transfer, the data may be processed by a controller established in a country where there is not an adequate level of protection of the privacy of individuals;

(b) the Data Exporter and the Data Importer agree to the adherence to the Clauses of another controller which thereby becomes a party to the Clauses and assumes the same obligations as the Data Importer.

Appendix 2 to Chapter 4

Example Privacy Policy

This is the privacy policy used by www.the-afs.com, the Association of Football Statisticians.

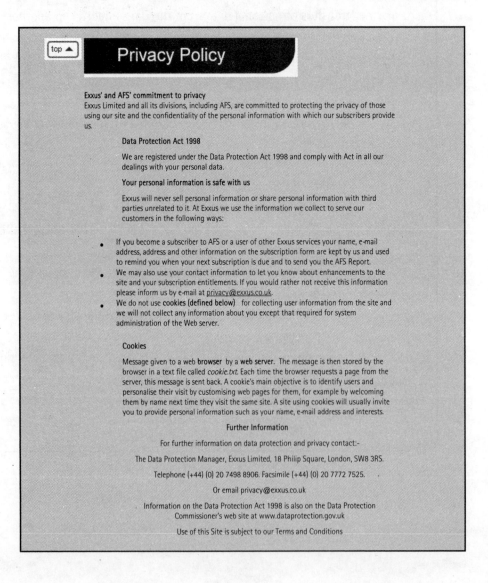

Privacy Policy

Exxus' and AFS' commitment to privacy
Exxus Limited and all its divisions, including AFS, are committed to protecting the privacy of those using our site and the confidentiality of the personal information with which our subscribers provide us.

Data Protection Act 1998

We are registered under the Data Protection Act 1998 and comply with Act in all our dealings with your personal data.

Your personal information is safe with us

Exxus will never sell personal information or share personal information with third parties unrelated to it. At Exxus we use the information we collect to serve our customers in the following ways:

- If you become a subscriber to AFS or a user of other Exxus services your name, e-mail address, address and other information on the subscription form are kept by us and used to remind you when your next subscription is due and to send you the AFS Report.
- We may also use your contact information to let you know about enhancements to the site and your subscription entitlements. If you would rather not receive this information please inform us by e-mail at privacy@exxus.co.uk.
- We do not use **cookies (defined below)** for collecting user information from the site and we will not collect any information about you except that required for system administration of the Web server.

Cookies

Message given to a web **browser** by a **web server**. The message is then stored by the browser in a text file called *cookie.txt*. Each time the browser requests a page from the server, this message is sent back. A cookie's main objective is to identify users and personalise their visit by customising web pages for them, for example by welcoming them by name next time they visit the same site. A site using cookies will usually invite you to provide personal information such as your name, e-mail address and interests.

Further Information

For further information on data protection and privacy contact:-

The Data Protection Manager, Exxus Limited, 18 Philip Square, London, SW8 3RS.

Telephone (+44) (0) 20 7498 8906. Facsimile (+44) (0) 20 7772 7525.

Or email privacy@exxus.co.uk

Information on the Data Protection Act 1998 is also on the Data Protection Commissioner's web site at www.dataprotection.gov.uk

Use of this Site is subject to our Terms and Conditions

Chapter 5

Where in the world?

Chapter 5

Where in the world?

Summary

· Whose laws apply?
· How to deal with jurisdiction issues on web sites
· Place of performance - practical advice
· Choosing jurisdiction
· Fighting international suits

The beauty of the internet as an advertising medium is that it can be reached from all corners of the globe. The photocopier, which in some quarters was regarded as a principal reason for the demise of communist regimes in Eastern Europe, has been replaced by the even more powerful medium of the internet for the dissemination of information.

However, there are more than 100 countries each with their own legal systems, and businesses selling goods and services over the internet can be fearful that they may fall foul of the laws of some obscure state where their web page can be accessed. Largely businesses should not worry. The financial benefits to be gained from ecommerce more than make up the largely minimal risks.

Whose laws apply

This chapter provides some guidance on the laws in this field and shows businesses how to address territorial issues when marketing on the internet.

Examples

1. The clothing company Land's End found it could not offer lifetime guarantees on its products because these breached German law. The case went to the German Supreme Court which, in 1999, held that the company could honour its guarantee but it was not allowed to tell German customers about it. German law also prohibited offering three goods for the price of two. American Express had also in Germany been forbidden from offering cardholders frequent flyer miles on each credit purchase. In July 2001, the Germans changed their laws principally because of pressure from internet retailers to remove these restrictions. The cases illustrate how global harmonisation of laws can occur because of international pressure arising from internet retailing.

2. US web site Yahoo! was ordered by a French court to bar all French users who might purchase Nazi memorabilia from the site - the sale of this type of material is allowed in the USA, but not in France.

Choosing which law applies

There are already long-established international rules on which law applies to international contracts. Many countries have signed the Rome and Lugano and Brussels Conventions. These, in general, state that people can choose to state in their contract which law applies and which courts will hear any dispute that arises. This is why most contracts drawn up by lawyers have a clause such as:

Choice of Law and Jurisdiction
This Agreement is subject to the laws of England and the parties agree to submit to the exclusive jurisdiction of the English courts in respect of any dispute under this Agreement. The place of performance of the contract shall be England.

In many cases, some other law is chosen, such as the laws of a particular US state, etc.

Even Scotland has different laws from England. There is no such thing as the law of the UK, so do not include such a reference in contract terms.

There are two separate issues here - which laws are applied and by which courts. The two do not necessarily go together, but it is sensible if they do. For example, the trial of the Lockerbie airline bombers was subject to Scottish law, but was held in the jurisdiction of the Netherlands. In most cases, it is too expensive to fly foreign lawyers into a different country so ensure the same law and jurisdiction apply.

However, not all 100+ countries of the world have chosen to agree to the international conventions, so in those cases there remains a risk that the country concerned will apply its own laws no matter what any contract terms say and even if all users of a web site have agreed clearly to accept the foreign law. This means no UK business can ever be 100 per cent certain it will win the day in arguing that its English or Scottish (etc.) choice of law and jurisdiction will apply.

In addition, where a matter of public policy arises, the courts may overturn a choice of law clause.

Choice of law example

Self-employed commercial agents paid on commission are entitled to strong protection under the EU agency directive. When they are sacked, they can often claim a large lump-sum in compensation. When an agent was sacked who worked in the EU, but his contract said Californian law applied (and no compensation for a sacked agent is available under Californian law), the European Court of Justice said EU agency law should prevail and the agent be entitled to compensation. (Ingmar GB Ltd v Eaton Leonard Technologies Inc. (ECJ 9.11.00, Case No. C-381/98), confirmed High Court 31 July 2001)

How to deal with jurisdiction issues on web sites

1. Make it very clear on the terms of use of the site, which must be clearly visible as 'Terms' on the home page or when people register to use the site, that English law and jurisdiction applies (or Scottish law, etc.).

2. Check whether the goods or services being supplied on the site can lawfully be sold in most of the major markets where buyers will be located. For example, anyone selling a product which might breach Muslim Sharia law might want to make it clear orders are not accepted from a particular territory which respects those laws.

3. Check if the trade mark used for selling the products and the domain name can be used in the major markets. It may be that goods cannot be sold under one name in, say, Australia, because someone else owns that trade mark there and this should be made clear on the web site. Chapter 3 looked at trade mark issues.

4. Consider the legal implications of translating the site into another language. The site may then be seen to be directed at the other state and it may be easier for the foreign laws to be applied.

5. Do not fight a jurisdiction case unless there is a lot of money at stake. They are complicated. Books on 'conflict of laws' are often 1000 pages long and whole university course modules are devoted to this topic alone. Be commercial. Settle if there are disputes. Take legal advice early on.

Jurisdiction regulation 44/2001

The European Commission adopted a regulation on jurisdiction and recognition and enforcement of judgments in civil and commercial matters that comes into force on 1 March 2002. The regulation deals with many jurisdiction issues, as well as those relevant to ecommerce. It provides that in the EU, generally, for commercial contracts people can choose in their contract terms which courts have jurisdiction. The regulation deals with where disputes are held, not which laws apply. So it relates to the jurisdiction, not choice of law issue.

It provides that people can be sued in the place of performance of a contract, where the dispute relates to a contract. It is important that those drafting contracts refer to the place of performance in their jurisdiction clauses - that the place of performance of the contract is England. It is by no means clear with goods bought on the internet where the place of performance is - where the goods are shipped from, where the server is located, where the goods are shipped to?

Place of performance - practical advice

Article 1(a) of regulation 44/2001 says that unless otherwise agreed, the place of performance for the sale of goods will be the place where, under the contract, the goods are to be delivered. So anyone selling goods on the internet who does not say where the place of performance is will find themselves left with the place of delivery as that place abroad. They may not want that to be the case and they should at least try to alter the position by a contract term. For services, the equivalent provision is where the services are provided. If a 'tort' such as misrepresentation or negligence occurs, then the courts where the harmful event occurred will have jurisdiction.

Special rules for consumer contracts

Under the regulation, there are special rules for consumer contracts. Most sellers on the internet want their own home state to have jurisdiction, not the state of the consumer who could be in any of the 15 EU states. The new regulation, however, says that if the seller has a commercial activity in the consumer's member state, or 'directs its activities' to that state, then that consumer's home state will handle disputes. The consumer is given a right to sue either where the consumer is based or in the supplier's territory. The supplier will not have such a choice.

Choosing jurisdiction

Some internet companies choose jurisdiction particularly carefully. Internet betting companies may choose to incorporate and operate offshore, particularly in tax havens, and certainly away from countries where gambling is banned or heavily regulated. Other companies with a product or service that cannot lawfully be sold in one country will choose a country where no such restrictions apply. Some countries have tried to attract internet companies in particular and offered special tax incentives if they base themselves in those territories.

Example - Sealand

The island of Sealand, a former wartime fort, off the Suffolk coast of the UK was annexed by an individual and independence declared. Due to ancient laws, by successfully fighting off British naval fire, its sovereignty is less open to challenge than might otherwise be the case. Little more than a rock at sea it offers itself as a haven for those seeking to avoid the worst legal regulatory environments of the world. The haven has operated since May 2000 (www.havenCo.com).

For most British businesses they will wish to choose English law and jurisdiction and include a clause to this effect in their online terms and conditions which are accessible on the web site. However, even then check the following:

Checklist

· Do the products comply with legislation in most major markets? Some products have to meet different standards in different countries. If there are countries where they may not be sold, say so on the web site.

· Is any distribution or supply contract in place that might prohibit sales outside a particular territory? Do such restrictions comply with the EU competition rules in regulation 2790/99, where applicable? The regulation permits exclusive distribution agreements in the EU, but dealers must not be prevented from passively supplying outside their exclusive territory. Having a web site is passive selling; a UK dealer could lawfully be prevented from sending a mass email or other mailing to a country outside its territory.

- Are the goods allowed to be sold under the same registered trade mark or trade name in all major markets serviced by the web site? Carry out trade mark searches and if someone else owns the same or similar name abroad, consider marketing under a different name in that territory.

- Will the goods be sold to consumers? If so, then remember the consumer will be allowed to bring any legal disputes to a local court.

- Is the product in a highly regulated area such as financial services, gambling or pharmaceuticals? If so, make sure detailed legal advice is taken in all major markets.

- Is the product illegal in some countries, for example, pornography or alcohol, or because it cannot be sold to people under the age of 18? If so, make sure the terms and conditions address this issue.

Fighting international suits

If a legal claim or a lawyer's letter arrives from another country, whether by post or email, the UK trader should seek legal advice immediately. There are probably time limits and if a reply is not given, a judgment may be entered and the trader's goods seized to enforce the judgment concerned.

The most important issue will be what are the merits of the case against the trader and how much money is at stake compared with the likely legal costs that may need to be expended to fight off the action. This cost/benefit analysis is crucial in all litigation.

Where sufficient money is at stake, then arguments over which courts have jurisdiction and indeed which laws apply may need to be run and be worth running.

Remember that rarely do jurisdiction issues cause problems and if terms and conditions deal with whose laws apply, in most cases traders have nothing to fear about the international nature and world-wide access of the internet.

Chapter 6

Getting business from the site

Chapter 6

Getting business from the site

Summary

· Attracting customers to the site
· Advertising laws
· Running a competition
· Points schemes
· Partnerships and alliances
· Linking and the law
· Example partnership agreement

Businesses with web sites need to tell customers that the site exists and ensure it is included on as many search engines as possible, so that when internet users make a search for a product, the site concerned is one of those that will be found.

Attracting customers to the site

Methods of attracting customers to your site include:

1. Put the web site address at the bottom of every email - 'Visit our web site at www.singlelaw.com', for example.

2. Make sure the site is interesting, has lots of useful content and is often updated so people will regularly visit.

3. Include the web site address on the company notepaper and other stationery and brochures.

4.   Add the web site address on general advertising in magazines, posters, etc.

5.   Register with as many search engines as possible or hire someone to do this for you.

6.   Consider buying several domain names, all leading to your site.

7.   Arrange mutual linking between yours and other sites where people interested in buying your goods or services may be online.

8.   Formal partnership agreements with other companies with related products that may direct traffic from their site to yours should be considered.

Advertising laws

The internet is not immune from laws that regulate advertisements. Make sure the accuracy of the site is thoroughly checked and that prices are up to date. Some companies have been prosecuted by trading standards authorities around the world, where prices are out of date or goods are misdescribed.

The following is a non-exhaustive list of the regulations to consider:

· Trade Descriptions Act - it is an offence to apply a false trade description to goods - for example, saying goods on the site are wool when they are nylon.

· Consumer Protection Act - it is unlawful to apply a misleading price indication to goods. Make sure prices are accurate and up to date.

· Sale of Goods Act 1979 - when goods are sold there is an implied condition that they will be of satisfactory quality and fit for their purpose. The EU consumer guarantees directive that comes into force in 2002 will provide very similar protection for consumers throughout the EU.

· Control of Misleading Advertisements Regulations - advertisements must not be misleading. Caution should be exercised when an advertisement compares one product with that of another company - the comparison must be fair, otherwise a breach of the Trade Marks Act 1994 may occur if the competitor's trade mark is used in the advertisement.

· Information Society Services Regulations 2001 - set out information about sellers on web sites which must be given.

When using an advertising agency, do not assume they will check that the words used comply with legislation. Always make sure there are contract terms setting out whose responsibility this is. For example, music or pictures used in an advertisement should only be used when permission from the copyright owner is obtained. Sometimes the agency simply gives the customer a right to use the material once. Just because the company is paying for the advertising work to be done, does not mean they will automatically own the copyright in what they have commissioned. If they want ownership of such rights, they should ensure the agency assigns the rights in a written contract.

Many web sites carry advertising from third party companies. It is a major revenue generator for the bigger sites. Sometimes no advertising fee is paid, but instead, mutual links are established - see partnership section below. In other cases, there is a simple arrangement with a fee paid. Both parties should draw up a written contract setting out the terms of the deal. The advertiser will want to ensure their logo and other details are displayed prominently, that links work, that no competitor is similarly allowed to advertise on the same page and/or site and that there is a right to terminate the arrangement on notice and in particular if hits are not high enough.

Example internet advertising - litigation

NMTV successfully obtained a court order for breach of the Competition Act 1998 against Jobserve. Jobserve told recruitment agencies that if they posted their vacancies on the NMTV jobs web site then they would not be able to use Jobserve. NMTV said this would mean no one would use its site as everyone would also want to use the well- known Jobserve site. The court, in a judgment in 2001, accepted there was a coherent argument to this effect and issued an interim injunction which ordered Jobserve not to exclude agencies who wanted to use NMTV as well. The Competition Act 1998 came into force on 1 March 2000 and prohibits anti- competitive agreements and abuses of a dominant position.

Running a competition

Many web sites offer those registering the opportunity to take part in a prize draw or other incentives for persuading friends and/or contacts to join. There are strict English laws on the running of competitions, so it is best to take advice from solicitors expert in the laws of lotteries and competitions. The rules should be clearly stated on the site as well.

If an incentive scheme is offered whereby people are paid or rewarded for drawing others into a network, then legislation in the Trading Schemes Act should be considered. Often, pyramid selling schemes, of which there are many on the internet, will infringe this legislation. Again, it is wise to take legal advice.

Points schemes

Many loyalty schemes operate on the internet. People gain points or money the more hits they make to a site or the more goods they buy at the site. Ensure the rules are clear and that it is also clarified as to how the scheme can be terminated and what happens to accumulated points in such a case. Not all countries allow such schemes, so it is sensible to take legal advice in the major markets that will be targeted.

Partnerships and alliances

Many partnership agreements are entered into between companies operating on the internet. Frequently, the parties agree that each will pay the other for business generated through the web site of the other. Technology can ensure that it can be relatively easily established when business comes through such a link.

There should be a written contract between the parties to the partnership arrangement. An example of such an agreement appears at the end of the chapter.

However, every commercial deal is different and readers should take their own legal advice.

Linking and the law

Normally there is no restriction on providing a link between web sites, although it is better practice to obtain consent from the party to whom the link will be made. However, if use of the site to which the link is to be formed is subject to online terms and conditions these are likely to be a 'contract'. One of those contract terms might prohibit linking without consent. In that case, the person forming a link without such consent may be in breach of the contract and could be restrained from so breaching the contract and be required to pay damages.

There is a large legal difference between a simple link and putting one's own heading above a third party's content. For example, if Singletons Solicitors has information about data protection laws on its web site, someone might link to that page of legal materials, usually without any legal problems. But, if that person makes the content appear beneath its own banner headlines then there may be a right to bring an action for 'passing off' (see Chapter 3), as users may believe that the material was generated by the company whose banner headings appear at the top.

Metatags

Sometimes companies put hidden words which are competitors' trade marks on their web site, so that people searching for Company Y's product are drawn to Company X's site. This amounts in the UK to use of a trade mark without consent and is not in accordance with honest practices as required by the Trade Marks Act 1994 and is an infringement of any UK registered trade mark, as case law has shown.

Appendix to Chapter 6

Example Partnership Agreement

Partnership Agreement
COMPANY.COM LIMITED

This Agreement is made on the date on the Schedule between:

(1)   COMPANY.com Limited, Company No. _____, whose principal place of business is at_____
('COMPANY'); and
(2)   _____ ('PARTNER').

BACKGROUND

A.   PARTNER is a company engaged in provision of _____.
B.   COMPANY is engaged in the business of _____.
C.   PARTNER has agreed to market and recommend the services of COMPANY as an inherent part of its software and COMPANY has agreed to set up a seamless connection from PARTNER software to allow users to _____ through COMPANY in return for which PARTNER shall be entitled to ___% of COMPANY's profits arising from such bookings on a monthly basis.
D.   COMPANY will market PARTNER software during its sales process and will be entitled to ___% of the licence fee as a one- off payment where COMPANY staff close such a deal.
E.   The parties have therefore agreed as follows:

Example Partnership Agreement (continued)

1. Definitions

'COMPANY's Site' means www.COMPANY.com.

'Confidential Information', 'Recipient' and 'Disclosing Party' are defined in clause 8.

'The Connection' is defined in clause 2.1.

'PARTNER COMPANY Customer' is defined in clause 3.1.

'PARTNER's Site' mean the web site or web sites of PARTNER described on the Schedule or such other replacement site(s) as PARTNER shall set up as successor from time to time.

'PARTNER Software' is defined in clause 2.1.

'Force Majeure Notice' is defined in clause 7.5.

2. Strategic Partnership, Connection And Marketing Obligations

2.1 PARTNER shall set up, with COMPANY's reasonable assistance where required, a connection within PARTNER software defined on the Schedule ('PARTNER Software') to the COMPANY Site which will provide a 'seamless' connection and enable PARTNER corporate customers to book _____ through COMPANY ('the Connection') directly from their own corporate intranet. Any special requirements for linking between COMPANY Site and PARTNER's Site are set out in full on the Schedule.

2.2 PARTNER and COMPANY shall be entitled to refer to each other as 'Strategic Alliance Partners' in their marketing and advertising.

2.3 PARTNER and COMPANY shall market the COMPANY products and the PARTNER software respectively during their marketing and sales processes to potential and existing customers with the aim of maximising sales of the other's products/services.

2.4 PARTNER shall notify COMPANY of any malfunctioning of the said connection or other problems with PARTNER's participation. COMPANY will respond promptly to all concerns upon notification by PARTNER.

Example Partnership Agreement (continued)

3. Commission - Company Payments to Partner

3.1 COMPANY agrees to pay to PARTNER a commission of _____% of COMPANY's gross profit, not including VAT, when COMPANY (or the _____ providers advertising on its Site) sells to a licensee or customer of the PARTNER Software via the Connection ('PARTNER COMPANY Customer') a _____.

3.2 COMPANY or its _____ providers shall have the sole right and responsibility for processing all orders made by PARTNER COMPANY Customers. PARTNER acknowledges that all agreements relating to sales to PARTNER COMPANY Customers shall be between COMPANY or its _____ providers and the Customer.

3.3 Prices for _____ will be set solely by COMPANY or its _____ providers in their discretion.

3.4 COMPANY shall identify customers originating from the PARTNER software and record them as 'PARTNER COMPANY Customers'.

3.5 COMPANY shall supply a monthly statement of all transactions with PARTNER COMPANY Customers during the previous calendar month. This will show all _____ sold, refunded or deferred with the PARTNER COMPANY Customers during the period of the statement. It will include details of the revenue and gross profit generated and calculation of all payments due to PARTNER.

3.6 COMPANY shall pay PARTNER after receipt of an invoice from PARTNER as provided below. PARTNER shall invoice COMPANY on the first day of each calendar month for the previous calendar month.

3.7 In no circumstances shall COMPANY be obliged to make any payments to PARTNER in relation to bookings for which full payment has not been made or in relation to which COMPANY has had to give a PARTNER COMPANY Customer a refund.

3.8 COMPANY shall use its reasonable endeavours to pay PARTNER within 30 days of the date of receipt of PARTNER invoice.

3.9 PARTNER agrees promptly to implement any request from COMPANY to remove,

Example Partnership Agreement (continued)

alter or modify any graphic or banner advertisement submitted by COMPANY that is being used by PARTNER at any time on the PARTNER Software or PARTNER Site.

4. Commission – Partner payments to company

4.1 PARTNER shall pay COMPANY a commission of ____% of the sale/licence price of PARTNER Software, not including VAT, where COMPANY has been instrumental in achieving or closing the sale/licence concerned.

4.2 Prices for PARTNER Software licences will be set solely by PARTNER in its discretion and COMPANY shall have not power or authority to bind PARTNER to any contract.

4.3 PARTNER shall supply a statement to COMPANY whenever it contracts with a customer for PARTNER Software in relation to which COMPANY has been involved. It will include details of the revenue generated from such contract and calculation of the __% payment due to COMPANY. This will be a one- off payment per sale. Where such customer places a future order with PARTNER COMPANY shall continue to be entitled to a __% payment for such repeat business.

4.4 PARTNER shall pay COMPANY after receipt of an invoice from COMPANY as provided below. COMPANY shall invoice PARTNER on receipt of the PARTNER contract details set out in clause 4.3.

4.5 In no circumstances shall PARTNER be obliged to make any payments to COMPANY in relation to a licence/contract for which payment has not been made.

4.6 PARTNER shall use its reasonable endeavours to pay COMPANY within 30 days of the date of receipt of COMPANY's invoice.

5. Term

5.1 This Agreement should remain in force from the date of this Agreement (or, if any, the date shown as the Effective Date on the Schedule) unless and until terminated on 30 days' written notice by one party to the other or otherwise as

Example Partnership Agreement (continued)

terminated below.

5.2 Either party may terminate this Agreement by notice in writing with immediate effect if the other party is in material breach of any of the terms of this Agreement and such breach, where it is remediable, remains unremedied 14 days after receipt of notice from the terminating party that the other party is in breach.

5.3 Either party shall have the right to terminate this Agreement with immediate effect on notice in writing if liquidation or similar proceedings are filed by or against the other party or if any action is taken by or against the other party under any law the purpose or effect of which is or may be to relieve such party in any manner from its debts or to extend the time of payment thereof or the other party makes an assignment for the benefit of creditors or makes any conveyance of any of its property which in the opinion of the terminating party may be to the detriment of that party's creditors or if a receiver or trustee or similar official is appointed with authority to take possession of the other party's property or any part thereof.

5.4 After termination each party shall pay the other commission due on sales the principal work for which was done prior to the date of termination and in the case of COMPANY it shall continue to pay PARTNER for orders from customers placed after the date of termination via the Connection for a period of 12 months thereafter. On termination the parties shall cease to call each other strategic partners and shall no longer have any obligation to market the other's products or services.

6. Ownership and Licences

6.1. Each party owns and shall retain all right, title and interest in its names, logos, trade marks, service marks, trade dress, copyrights and proprietary technology, including, without limitation, those names, logos, trade marks, service marks,

Example Partnership Agreement (continued)

trade dress, copyrights and proprietary technology currently used or which may be developed and/or used by it in the future including in all materials on its own site.

6.2. Each party grants to the other a revocable, non-exclusive, worldwide licence to use, reproduce and transmit the name, logos, trade marks, trade dress and proprietary technology, as designated on the Schedule on their respective sites solely for the purpose of creating links between Sites and PARTNER Software. Except as expressly set forth in this Agreement or permitted by applicable law, neither party may copy, distribute, modify, reverse engineer or create derivative works from the other party's works. Neither party may sublicense, assign or transfer any such licences for the use of the other party's works, and any attempt at such sublicence, assignment or transfer is void.

6.3. Each party grants the other a non- exclusive, worldwide, royalty- free licence to use, reproduce and transmit any graphic or banner advertisement submitted by the other solely for co-branding purposes. Each party will remove such graphic or banner advertisement upon request by the other party.

7.   Liability and Exclusions

7.1. Each party represents to the other that (a) it has the authority to enter into this Agreement and sufficient rights to grant any licences granted hereby, and (b) any material that is provided to the other party and displayed on the other party's site will not (i) infringe on any third party's copyright, patent, trade mark, trade secret or other proprietary rights or right of publicity or privacy; (ii) violate any applicable law, statute, ordinance or regulation; (iii) be defamatory or libellous; (iv) be lewd, pornographic or obscene; (v) violate any laws regarding unfair competition, anti- discrimination or false advertising; (vi) promote violence or contain hate speech; or (vii) contain viruses, time bombs or other similar harmful or deleterious programming routines.

Example Partnership Agreement (continued)

7.2 Except for the above representations neither party makes any representations or warranties to the other party, including, but not limited to, any implied warranties of satisfactory quality or fitness for a particular purpose.

7.3 Each party hereby agrees to indemnify, defend and hold harmless the other party and its affiliates, directors, officers, employees and agents, from and against any and all liability, claims, losses, damages, injuries or expenses (including reasonable attorneys' fees) brought by a third party, arising out of a breach, or alleged breach, of any of its representations or obligations herein.

7.4 In no event shall either party be liable to the other party for any indirect, special, exemplary, consequential or incidental damages, whether arising from breach of contract or liability in tort. Each party's liability to the other, including without limitation, for direct loss arising from breach of this Agreement or otherwise shall be limited to the total sum it has paid the other party in commission hereunder in the calendar year of the date of claim. Nothing in this Agreement shall exclude or limit either party's liability for death or personal injury to the other arising from its negligence.

7.5 Neither party shall be liable to the other for any failure to perform its obligations pursuant to this Agreement where such failure is caused by an event beyond the control of the party in default ('a Force Majeure Event'), provided that

    (a)   any party seeking to rely on this provision shall give written notice ('the Force Majeure Notice') to the other containing full particulars of the event which it claims is a Force Majeure Event;

    (b)   this clause shall cease to apply if the Force Majeure Event no longer prevents the performance of the obligations of the party in default within 90 days of the date of the Force Majeure Notice.

If the Force Majeure Event continues to prevent the performance of the obligations of the party in default for a period of more than 90 days from

Example Partnership Agreement (continued)

the date of the Force Majeure Notice, then both parties shall be relieved of any further obligation arising out of this Agreement.

8. Confidentiality

8.1 Either Party (the 'Disclosing Party') may from time to time disclose Confidential Information to the other party (the 'Recipient'). 'Confidential Information' is all non- public information concerning the business, technology, internal structure and strategies of the Disclosing Party which is conveyed to the Recipient orally or in tangible form and is either marked as 'confidential' or which is identified as 'confidential' prior to disclosure. The Recipient will keep in confidence and trust and will not disclose or disseminate, or permit any employee, agent or other person working under Recipient's direction to disclose or disseminate, the existence, source, content or substance of any Confidential Information to any other person without limit as to time.

8.2 Recipient will employ at least the same methods and degree of care, but no less than a reasonable degree of care, to prevent disclosure of the Confidential Information as Recipient employs with respect to its own confidential patent data, trade secrets and proprietary information.

8.3 Recipient's employees and independent contractors will be given access to the Confidential Information only on a need-to-know basis, and only if they have executed a form of non- disclosure agreement with Recipient which imposes a duty to maintain the confidentiality of information identified or described as confidential by Recipient and after Recipient has expressly informed them of the confidential nature of the Confidential Information.

8.4 Recipient will not copy or load any of the Confidential Information onto any computing device or store the Confidential Information electronically except in circumstances in which Recipient has taken all reasonable precautions to prevent access to the information stored on such device or electronic storage

Example Partnership Agreement (continued)

facility by anyone other than the persons entitled to receive the Confidential Information hereunder.

8.5 The commitments in this Clause 8 will not impose any obligations on Recipient with respect to any portion of the received information which: (i) is now generally known or available or which, hereafter through no act or failure to act on the part of Recipient, becomes generally known or available; (ii) is rightfully known to Recipient at the time of receiving such information; (iii) is furnished to Recipient by a third party without restriction on disclosure and without Recipient having actual notice or reason to know that the third party lacks authority to so furnish the information; (iv) is independently developed by Recipient; or (v) is required to be disclosed by operation of law or by an instrumentality of the government, including but not limited to any court, tribunal or administrative agency.

9. General

9.1 Assignment: Neither party shall without the consent in writing of the other party assign or transfer any of its obligations or rights hereunder.

9.2 Entire agreement: This Agreement embodies the entire understanding and agreement between the parties in connection with the subject matter of this Agreement and neither party is relying on any representations, promises, terms, conditions or obligations oral or written express or implied other than those contained herein. Neither party seeks to exclude liability for fraudulent or grossly negligent misrepresentation.

9.3 Waiver: No waiver by either party of any term hereof shall constitute a waiver of any such term in any other case whether prior or subsequent thereto.

9.4 Amendment: This Agreement shall not be modified or amended except by agreement in writing by an authorised representative of each of the parties.

9.5 Headings: The clause headings in this Agreement are for reference purposes only

Example Partnership Agreement (continued)

and are not intended to be taken into account when interpreting the clauses.

9.6 Notices: All notices or other communications relating to this Agreement shall be given in writing addressed to the addressed on page 1 and the schedule, by personal delivery, courier, post or fax, and shall be deemed to have been received:

(a) in the case of a letter, on the date shown on a receipt of certificate of delivery, if the letter is delivered personally, or sent by pre-paid courier or registered or certified mail to the then-current business address of the party and the person effecting delivery obtains a receipt or himself signs a certificate of delivery showing the date of delivery, or

(b) in the case of a fax, on the date of sending as shown on the sender's copy of the fax, if the fax is sent to the recipient's then- current fax number, a successful transmission report is generated by the fax machine, there is no evidence of a failed transmission, and a copy is sent at the same time using one of the methods above, or

(c) whatever the means of delivery, on the date indicated in any acknowledgement of receipt, if the recipient acknowledges in writing directly or indirectly that the notice has been received.

The relevant postal address, postal box and fax numbers of the parties shall be as above or most recently notified. Either party may, by at least fifteen (15) days notice to the other party, change its business address, postal box or fax numbers. Communication shall thereafter be sufficiently given if sent as provided to the destinations specified in such notice of change.

9.7 Law and Jurisdiction: Each party irrevocably agrees that the courts of England shall have non- exclusive jurisdiction to resolve any controversy or claim of whatever nature arising out of or relating to this Agreement or breach thereof, and that the laws of England shall govern such controversy or claim. The place of performance shall be England.

Example Partnership Agreement (continued)

IN WITNESS the parties have signed this Agreement on the last page.

THE SCHEDULE

Date Agreement made_____2001

Partner Name

_____

Address:_____

Tel:_____

Fax:_____

www:_____

Email:_____

Contact Name:_____

PARTNER software which will be connected to the COMPANY Site:

_____

COMPANY web site: www.COMPANY.com

PARTNER web site(s): www._____

COMPANY trade marks, etc. which PARTNER may use in its software and how they may be used

_____

_____

Special requirements for linking (e.g. to home page only, etc.)_____

Effective Date (if any):_____

Signatures

1. Signed by_____   Name_____Signature

    Title_____

Example Partnership Agreement (continued)

For and on behalf of
COMPANY.com Limited

In the presence of:
Witness_____ Signature
Name_____
Address_____
Occupation_____

2.   Signed by_____ Name _____Signature
Title_____
For and on behalf of
_____

In the presence of:
Witness_____ Signature
Name_____
Address_____
Occupation_____

DATE OF LAST SIGNATURE_____2001
(Being the date of this Agreement)

Chapter 7

Online contracts

Chapter 7

Online contracts

Summary

· Legislation
· Electronic contracts
· Terms and conditions – making the contract stick
· TrustUK
· Web Trader
· Distance selling regulations
· Credit card transactions
· Example online conditions of sale

The US Census Bureau of the Department of Commerce estimated US retail ecommerce sales for the third quarter of 2000 were $6.373 billion. The second quarter estimate was $5.526 billion. Total retail sales for third quarter 2000 were estimated at $812.0 billion (see www.census.gov/mrts/www/current.html). This shows how important online contracts are. Businesses that shy away from doing business in this way will lose revenue. The legal risks are small by comparison.

English law is wonderfully adapted to electronic commerce. To form a contract the legal rule has always been that all that is required is an offer, which is accepted, consideration (usually a price) and an intention to create legal relations. With a few exceptions, the written word has never been needed; verbal contracts are enforced every day.

An email is much better than the average telephone order. Terms and conditions can be thrust at the buyer, who cannot proceed to purchase until they are accepted. The buyer can print the conditions. Full emailed details about delivery charges and the goods themselves can be easily and cheaply supplied to the customer. Telephone selling is nothing like as easy, or as certain, or as provable. Not surprisingly, the

European Commission wants all EU states to enable contracts to be formed easily in this way and has issued new EU laws in directives on electronic signatures and electronic commerce, so that all EU states will ultimately allow contracts to be formed in this way. In England, it was always the case.

Even in England, there have been some areas of law where 'writing' on a piece of paper is required, such as for sales of houses and assignments of copyright and even there the laws will be changed to allow electronic signature.

This chapter looks at online contracts and some of the issues that arise. It includes an example of some online conditions of sale of goods at the end of the chapter.

Legislation

The table below summarises recent EU ecommerce legislation and also shows which UK regulations implement the various EU directives set out there.

Name	Details
EU distance selling directive 97/7. In force in the UK from 31.10.00 by the Consumer Protection (Distance Selling) Regulations 2000 SI 2000/2334.	1. Applies to sales of goods and services to consumers only (not business buyers). 2. Gives consumers rights to cancel most contracts on 7 days' notice (3 months' notice in some cases). 3. Requires certain information to be given to consumers, to appear on the web site.
EU electronic signature directive 1999/93 (published EU Commission's Official Journal 19.1.2000, L13/12). In force in the UK from July 2000 by Electronic Communications Act 2000; will be followed by further regulations.	1. Provides for recognition throughout EU of electronic signatures and electronic contracts. 2. Will aid ecommerce in the UK and elsewhere between individuals and the government.

EU and UK ecommerce regulations

Name	Details
EU electronic commerce directive 2000/31 (published OJ L178/1 17.7.2000). Must be implemented throughout the EU by 17 January 2002. In August 2001, the DTI issued a consultation document on implementation of the directive (see DTI web site www.dti.gov.uk). The Information Society Services Regulations 2001 will implement the directive.	1. Requires important contractual information to be provided when buying online, such as telling customers how a contract is formed (article 10). 2. Requires all member states to permit electronic contracts. 3. Deals with liability of internet service providers, who will normally escape liability for the content of material transmitted using their services if they remove offending material expeditiously as soon as a problem arises.
Regulation on jurisdiction and judgments 44/2001 on jurisdiction and recognition and enforcement of judgments in civil and commercial matters (22 December 2000, OJ L12/1 16.1.2001). Comes into force on 1 March 2002 (see Chapter 5).	1. Sets out which courts have jurisdiction for disputes. 2. For web sales to consumers, the consumer will be free to sue in their local court, no matter what law the contract provides. 3. Local arbitration services will be set up.
Regulation of Investigatory Powers Act 2000 and the regulations made under it - The Telecommunications (Lawful Business Practice) (Interception of Communications) Regulations 2000 (SI 2000/2699). In force from 24 October 2000 (Not an EU harmonisation measure).	1. The RIPA sets out when electronic communications can be intercepted (such as by the police). 2. The regulations allow employers and others to intercept emails and telephone calls without consent of an employee, in many cases. 3. However, compliance with data protection law is also necessary.

EU and UK ecommerce regulations (continued)

Name	Details
Data Protection Act 1998, which implemented the EU data protection directive (95/46) from 1 March 2000 (see Chapter 4).	1. Requires personal data such as many email addresses, names and addresses, details of purchasing habits on web sites, etc. to be handled in accordance with eight data protection principles and for businesses to register (notify) their holding of such data. 2. In the ecommerce field, in many cases therefore a privacy policy on a web site is advisable, to set out what will be done with personal data gathered on the site. 3. See also the draft Data Protection Code of Practice for Employer/Employee Relationships (October 2000), published by the Information Commissioner, which includes important provisions on surveillance of employee emails and related areas. 4. See also rights of subject access to information in emails, under section 7 of the Act set out in Guidance of the Commissioner and the separate guidance for data controllers and for consumers, on the use of the internet and data protection of the Commissioner.

EU and UK ecommerce regulations (continued)

Electronic contracts

An electronic contract is, simply, one formed electronically. For example, Mr A may email Mr B and offer to sell his car to him for £5,000. Mr B may accept the offer by return email. Provided all the details are clear, they have thus formed a contract.

Many large businesses have done business together using direct electronic links for many years and have codes of practice/conduct in place between them setting out how those systems will operate.

This chapter examines the contracts formed when goods or services are available to purchase on a web site where the consumer supplies their credit card or debit card details to purchase online, and a contract is made in that way.

Electronic signatures

The Electronic Communications Act 2000 made it clear under English law that contracts formed electronically are valid (which was usually the case before the law changed in any event). It also made provision for 'electronic signatures'. These are not handwritten signatures scanned into a computer. Instead, they are a security device people can buy by producing proof of ID, resulting in them being supplied with a CD to load into their computer and then they are sent in the post a PIN number or code word to get the system operating. Once in operation, they can send emails or sign contracts which are 'digitally signed'. It means the sender is more likely to be who they say they are. However it is not 100 per cent foolproof.

Traders can file their VAT returns online in the UK if they have such an electronic signature and it is likely this is an area which will expands over the next few years. Many companies have set themselves up offering electronic signatures for sale.

In 2001, the Government was consulting on full implementation of the EU directive on electronic signatures (see www.dti.gov.uk/cii/ecommerce/europeanpolicy/esigncondoc.pdf).

The directive requires certain specified and approved trusted third parties to approve the issuing of electronic signatures.

Terms and conditions – making the contract stick

A trader wanting to sell goods or services from a web site needs to ensure they draw up a set of terms and conditions for supply of the goods or services. An example appears at the end of this chapter. However, every trader operates in a different way and legal advice should ideally be sought before any terms are used. Sometimes altering one word or clause can have a dramatic effect. For example, no terms can exclude liability for death, on account of provisions in the Unfair Contract Terms Act 1977. If the terms try to do so, an entire clause which limits liability in other ways may be void.

A huge amount of business is now undertaken electronically. In the UK, ecommerce transactions in 1999 were worth £2.8 billion (Cabinet Office report ecommerce@its.best.uk).

Distance selling legislation (see below) requires that buyers from web sites who are consumers must be given certain basic contractual and other information, so traders need terms and conditions for this and other reasons.

Just as important as the terms, is ensuring they are on the right place on the web site so that they are seen and ideally accepted before the consumer purchases. It is better if they can be viewed generally before a purchaser proceeds down a chain of clicks that leads to a purchase and in addition that they appear before the point when the consumer commits to buying the goods or services concerned. The consumer should ideally be allowed to print the conditions and save them to a hard drive for future reference. Best practice is to have the consumer click to indicate that the terms are accepted.

The terms and conditions will deal with issues such as returns of the goods if they are defective, delivery charges, import duties (if they are being imported from abroad), substitutes, warranties, exclusions of liability, etc.

Online terms and conditions are available on most web sites where goods or services are supplied. It is therefore incredibly easy to find examples of the terms used on other sites. Copying those terms will be a breach of the Copyright, Designs and Patents Act 1988 and make the business copying a potential competitor's conditions look ridiculous when such plagiarism is discovered, but there is nothing to stop a company taking any of the ideas for types of clauses from another site and then producing their own set. Remember that foreign law contracts may not be appropriate for England and Wales or Scotland and that the products are very relevant to the terms, so they may need modification. Terms and conditions for downloading software online, for example, will not be anything like terms and conditions for the purchase of a book from a web site.

TrustUK

TrustUK is a non-profit making UK body, endorsed by the British Government, helping to give consumers confidence when they buy online. Trust UK says:

'What does it mean to me when I buy online?'

A webtrader showing the TrustUK hallmark operates to a high level of commercial standards designed to:

· protect your privacy;

· ensure that your payments are secure;

· helping you to make an informed buying decision;

· let you know what you have agreed to - and how to cancel orders should you need to;

· deliver the goods or services ordered within the agreed time period;

· protect children;

· sort out any complaints, wherever you live.

Companies seeking to sell goods or services online will find it advantageous to be a member of a scheme such as this. There are others which operate, but it is best to choose one which is well-recognised and has Government approval.

'Web Trader'

A similar scheme operated by the Consumers' Association is 'Which? Web Trader' of which there are over 1,500 members. The Which? Web Trader scheme is also part of TrustUK and the symbols displayed by those who meet the requirements include the Web Trade sign and also the TrustUK sign. The following is the description of the scheme.

Further information is at http://whichwebtrader.which.net/webtrader/index.html, an extract of which is shown on the following page. (Please check current web pages, as this site is constantly updated.)

WHICH?nline
www.which.net

 WHICH? WEB TRADER SCHEME
ABOUT US | ABOUT THE SCHEME | ASSOCIATES | AFFILIATES

Search

I am looking for..

`GO`

List all traders
Shopping Partners

Go Shopping

Accessories
Art
Auto
Books & Magazines
Computers
Department Stores
Electronics & Cameras
Entertainment
Fashion
Finance & Property
Food & Drink
Gifts & Flowers
Health & Beauty
Home & Garden
Music
Sports
Toys, Babies & Kids
Travel

Which? Web Trader - What the scheme means for traders

Consumer confidence is the key to successful Internet trading. If you are a UK-based organisation and want to do business on the Internet, our scheme could help you trade more successfully. Our logo will give consumers confidence in your service. But can your business meet our standards?

To be a Which? Web Trader and to display the Which? Web Trader logo, you need to tell us about your business. Our lawyers will check the details you provide. You also need to agree to meet the conditions of our **Code of Practice** for web traders. Our current list of traders can be found **here.**

Our Code is designed to make sure consumers get a fair deal and to provide them with protection if things go wrong. We've explained the benefits of the scheme for consumers **here.**

To join our scheme, please fill in this form and send it to our legal department. Membership of the scheme is absolutely free. We do not charge for this service.

We will notify you by e-mail when we have finished checking your details and provide you with our Which? Web Trader logo to display on your site. See the **application guide** for more information about how to apply.

If you are authorised to display the Which? Web Trader logo, you must do the following:

Display the logo prominently on your web site, so it can be seen by visitors entering your site, using the code provided by us.

Display the text 'We belong to the Which? Web Trader Code of Practice' adjacent to the logo.

Not change the logo in any way.

Not say or suggest in any way that Which? or Consumers' Association or any of its associated companies recommends your products.

The logo belongs to Which? Limited. We only give you permission to display it on the website of your registered business and not in any other place.

You may use the logo in your print advertising. If you do you must include the words:

We are a Which? Web Trader
www.which.net/webtrader

What Which? will do

We will check the information supplied by you. If there is any information that you do not want passed to consumers please tell us.

When both the legal requirements and the site requirements have been met we will add your company's name to the list of traders on our site.

If we receive complaints from consumers about your service, we will investigate and may withdraw our permission for you to display our logo.

You will be told of the complaint before we make a final decision and you will have the chance to reply. Where appropriate, we will give you the chance to put things right. If we find that you have not kept to our Code, we may decide to exclude you from the scheme. If we do decide to exclude you, we will tell you so in writing and at the same time will give you details of how to appeal against our decision. Following any appeal, our decision will be final.

We will publicise the scheme when we launch it and on an ongoing basis.

We reserve the right to make minor changes to the Code. You will always be able to see the most up-to-date version online at **Code of Practice.**

What the scheme will not do

This scheme and the use of a logo on a site does not suggest we recommend the goods or services you are offering, or the customer service you provide outside the areas covered in the Code.

What the consumer will see

A description of the scheme and the code.

The consumer will see your name and URL (address) on the list of traders who have agreed to follow the Which? Web Trader code of practice and comply with its requirements.

Contact us:
e-mail: webtrader@which.net
phone: 01992 822 888
fax: 0207 770 7485 (mark 'Webtrader')
post: Which? Web Trader, Castlemead, Gascoyne Way, Hertford X, SG14 1YB

Distance Selling Regulations

All businesses selling goods and services from a web site in the EU to consumers (not other businesses) need to comply with the EU Distance Selling Directive 97/7. In the UK, this was brought into force by the Distance Selling Regulations on

31 October 2000. The regulations do two things: (i) they require consumers to be given certain information about the seller, rights to cancel the contract, etc., and (ii) the consumer is given a right to cancel the contract after it is made and whether or not there is anything wrong with the goods or services. Not all contracts can be cancelled.

Lots of information on the regulations is on the Department of Trade and Industry distance selling web site at www.dti.gov.uk/cacp/ca/dsdbulletin.htm.

The regulations do not apply to all distance contracts; the most important exception is for financial services (a separate proposed directive on the distance marketing of financial services is currently being discussed).

The list of means of distance communications which is caught by the Directive includes:

Indicative list of means of distance communication

1. Unaddressed printed matter. The Mail Order Transactions (Information) Order 1976 is replaced by these new regulations.
2. Addressed printed matter.
3. Letters.
4. Press advertising with order forms.
5. Catalogues.
6. Telephone with human intervention.
7. Telephone without human intervention (automatic calling machine, audiotext).
8. Radio.
9. Videophones (telephone with screen).
10. Videotext (microcomputer and television screen) with keyboard or touch screen.
11. Electronic mail.
12. Facsimile machines (fax).
13. Television (teleshopping).

Clearly selling from a web site is a 'distance' communication under this provision.

Exclusions include any contract:

(a) for the sale or other disposition of an interest in land, except for a rental agreement;

(b) for the construction of a building where the contract also provides for a sale or other disposition of an interest in land on which the building is constructed, except for a rental agreement;

(c) relating to financial services, a non-exhaustive list of which is contained in Schedule 2 of the regulations and includes:

    1. investment services;

    2. insurance and reinsurance operations;

    3. banking services;

    4. services relating to dealings in futures or options.

(d) concluded by means of an automated vending machine or automated commercial premises;

(e) concluded with a telecommunications operator through the use of a public pay-phone;

(f) concluded at an auction (so internet auctions are also excluded).

The major provisions of the Directive do not apply to contracts for the provision of accommodation, transport, catering or leisure services, where the supplier undertakes, when the contract is concluded, to provide these services on a specific date or within a specific period. So, anyone buying air tickets online, for example, has no right to cancel.

Exclusions

There are many exclusions both from the regulations and from the right to cancel in the regulations. All traders therefore should read the regulations carefully to check whether and how they apply to them.

Rights

The regulations give consumers:

1. The right to receive clear information about the goods or services before deciding to purchase.

2. Confirmation of this information in writing or in another appropriate durable medium, e.g. fax or email. The Directive on which the regulations are based requires that the consumer be given information in writing or another 'durable medium that is available and accessible to him'. It does not say exactly what this means, so the DTI takes the view that email is a durable medium in the sense that it is open to the consumer to retain the information. Giving the details verbally is not, however, enough.

3. A cooling-off period of seven working days, in which the consumer can withdraw from the contract (for sales of goods, this is seven working days from the day after the goods are delivered). The statutory right of withdrawal below does not apply where:

    (a)   for the supply of services if the supplier has complied with regulation 8(3) and performance of the contract has begun with the consumer's agreement before the end of the cancellation period applicable under regulation 12;

    (b)   for the supply of goods or services, the price of which is dependent on fluctuations in the financial market which cannot be controlled by the supplier;

(c)   for the supply of goods made to the consumer's specifications or clearly personalised or which by reason of their nature cannot be returned or are liable to deteriorate or expire rapidly;

(d)   for the supply of audio or video recordings or computer software, if they are unsealed by the consumer;

(e)   for the supply of newspapers, periodicals or magazines; or

(f)   for gaming, betting or lottery services.

The cooling-off period is three months where the supplier has not given notice of the seven-day period to the customer. This is one reason why terms and conditions should be altered to allow for this. This point illustrates the importance for businesses in amending their terms and conditions now, to cover these new rights, so that the legal position can to some extent be ameliorated.

The effect of a notice of cancellation is that the contract shall be treated as if it had not been made.

Regulation 8(3) says:

Subject to regulation 9, prior to the conclusion of a contract for the supply of services, the supplier shall inform the consumer in writing or in another durable medium which is available and accessible to the consumer that, unless the parties agree otherwise, he will not be able to cancel the contract under regulation 10 once the performance of the services has begun with his agreement.

Delivery in 30 days

Unless agreed otherwise with the supplier, there is a right to receive goods or services within 30 days. This accords with the period that is usual in the mail order industry, in any event.

Action for companies

· Check if the regulations apply to the particular business.

· Are the goods or services excluded?

· Are the sales to consumers rather than businesses?

· Assuming the regulations apply, check that the correct information is given to consumers.

· Check compliance with other requirements such as 30-day delivery dates.

· Ensure the right to cancel is implemented.

· Take legal advice in cases of doubt.

Credit card transactions

Most companies selling goods or services over the internet will require the consumer to provide a credit or debit card number. This should be done on a secure part of the site or it is unlikely the consumer will be prepared to give those details. In any event, the consumer should ideally be given access to further information on the site about how the details provided will be kept confidential.

Security

Traders will need to enter into a contract with the relevant credit card company who have standard agreements for this purpose, before being entitled to offer payment by card on accounts.

Businesses may also like to consider giving consumers a telephone number they can ring, fax number, email contact or even a postal address if they would prefer to place their order that way. This can certainly help maximise business/orders for smaller, growing businesses. Large internet trading companies may not be happy to have such a mixture of means of communication.

Example

The Data Protection Act 1998 requires those controlling personal data to keep it safe and secure and it is very bad publicity for any business to find that its security procedures are breached. In 2000, a teenager caused £2m of damage through computer hacking, and managed to obtain Bill Gates' (of Microsoft) credit card details and order a consignment of Viagra for him. Criminal proceedings were brought against him under the Computer Misuse Act 1990. Raphael Gray had obtained access to 23,000 credit cards and targeted companies telling them their online security was inadequate. One company went out of business and Visa spent £250,000 monitoring accounts in consequence. US and UK police assumed he would be a major player, one of the mafia or some other body, and tracked him to a home in Carmarthen in South Wales, where they found he was a teenager acting alone. He has been placed on probation after evidence was heard that he had a mental disorder and low self- esteem. He is now working for a computer software company.

Summary

Goods or services can easily be sold from a web site. English law enables such contracts to be fully enforceable. It is important to have terms and conditions on the web site and to ensure that legislation such as the distance selling regulations is followed. Agreements will also need to be signed with a credit or debit card company and of course in the normal way with manufacturers or suppliers of the goods and/or services that are resold on the site, where applicable.

Appendix 1 to Chapter 7

Example Online Conditions of Sale

Our terms and conditions apply to all online conditions of sale from our web site. The terms are set out below. Read them before ordering. You may wish to print a copy for future reference. Other terms and conditions on our site such as our privacy policy should also be read as part of this agreement. We may change these terms from time to time without notice to you. Changes will apply to any subsequent orders received.

1. We reserve the right to change these terms from time to time. Changes will be posted on this site.

2. We agree to sell you the goods for the price stated. We deliver to UK addresses only. No goods are left unless an adult signs for delivery.

3. Delivery charges and when we estimate we may supply the goods to you are contained in our separate Delivery section of the site (see Delivery [LINK]). We try to deliver goods when stated but cannot guarantee delivery by such date. Time is not of the essence.

4. Goods are subject to availability and if we cannot supply them we will inform you and you will be given a full refund of what you have paid.

5. The goods are sold at the price on our web site at the date we receive the order from you. If we find a pricing error on our web site we will inform you as soon as possible and give you the opportunity, if you wish, of reconfirming your order at the correct price or cancelling it. If we cannot contact you we will cancel the order. If you cancel and you have paid for the goods, you will be given a full refund.

Example Online Conditions of Sale (continued)

6. Payment can be made by any means set out in our Delivery [LINK] terms. We aim to keep details of your order and payment secure (click here to see our Security Policy [LINK]); however, except in cases of negligence, we are not liable for any losses caused as a result of unauthorised access to information provided by you.

7. The contract between us shall be governed by the laws of England and Wales and any dispute between us will be resolved exclusively in the courts of England and Wales.

8. If you receive faulty goods we handle this in accordance with our Returns policy [LINK].

9. Where applicable, you may cancel your order under the distance selling regulations (see the Returns policy [LINK]) for further information and then we collect the goods from you without charge to you.

Chapter 8

Employee email and internet policies

Chapter 8
Employee email and internet policies

Summary

· Use of email and internet at work
· Legal requirements for emails
· Sample email notice
· Liability for employers
· Privacy laws and surveillance
· Sacking email and internet abusers
· Example employee email policy

One of the greatest changes in office life in the last 10 years has been the move to email. Many office workers now spend most of their day in front of a personal computer and many have access to email and the internet. In many businesses, email has replaced fax and letters and to some extent the telephone as the primary means of communications.

Use of email and the internet at work

In most cases this change is a good thing. Email is cheaper than long-distance telephone calls. It can be quicker. There is a permanent record of what was said. It can carry dangers of employees wasting time online, committing to email statements which may carry liability (such as defamatory words or material which breaches copyright or obscenity laws) and employees acting too quickly without the thought they might give to a formal letter. However, in general, the advantages outweigh the disadvantages.

The law does not cause too many problems either. The Regulation of Investigatory Powers Act 2000 and regulations made under it on lawful business practice allow most employers to supervise employees by intercepting their emails and telephone calls lawfully, without employee consent, as long as the employees know this is going on. Most employers, however, should consider having a standard notice on emails - see below - and an email and internet policy for employees, so they know where they stand. If employers do this, then there are unlikely to be many legal problems.

The first issue for employers is often whether to allow employees to use the internet at work or not. A standard question the author asks at legal IT conferences at which she speaks is, 'Who has an employee internet policy?' and 'Who allows all employees access to the internet at work?'. The answers vary widely. The larger UK plcs with tens of thousands of employees will often have very strict, inflexible, policies and may restrict access severely or even ban it altogether. Smaller businesses typically trust employees more or do not have the need for a detailed policy and allow more access. Some companies positively encourage employees to get to know how to use email and the internet and are pleased staff will book a holiday online at work, rather than queuing in a travel agent's for an hour and arrive back late from lunch. In other companies, that is a sackable offence. Neither attitude is right or wrong, but in law, the important issue is making all employees know where they stand.

The Trades Union Congress recommends that employers of unionised workforces enter into agreements with the union about what type of surveillance is to be instigated - see the report at www.tuc.org.uk/law/tuc-2684-f0.cfm.

Employers in general should consider consulting with employees, as this is as much a psychological as a legal issue. Staff who feel they are not trusted and their every move being watched are unlikely to work as well as those who feel their personal autonomy is unchallenged. However, some of the legal risks employees can foist on their employer through unsupervised use of the internet and email mean that surveillance in many cases is advisable.

Legal requirements for email

The Companies Act 1985 and Business Names Act 1985 require that company/business notepaper and invoices should carry certain statutory information. It is not clear, though, if an email is a business letter in the same category as a piece of paper. No legal case has yet decided the issue. It is possible, therefore, that companies need put no corporate type information on an email.

However, all the bigger UK companies do so; it looks more professional and just as important it ensures that the recipient of the email is given information such as the telephone number of the other party. Business can be lost because the telephone number does not appear. Not everyone wants to respond by email; 95 per cent of the correspondence which the author receives from clients of her law firm is now by email. It is very frustrating if there is no document on the file that gives the contact details. Also, companies spend thousands of pounds on their corporate image and logos and notepaper designs and then let employees send emails out in any format they like - it is not good for branding to allow such differences.

The requirements under the legislation described above include:

· Full company name including whether the company is Ltd, plc, limited liability partnership or sole trader (in which case the trading name and individual trader's name or partners' names should appear). The EU Electronic Commerce Directive and Information Society Services Regulations 2001 also require such information to be given.

· Registered office address for limited companies (or general address for unincorporated businesses).

· Registered company number (where applicable). This can be found by searching any company name in the UK at www.companieshouse.gov.uk in a matter of seconds.

· Place of incorporation of the company.

In addition, it is sensible to give the following:

· Telephone and fax number

· Full name and surname of person sending the email and their job title

· Company web site details

If secret information is sent by email, then to impose an obligation of confidence the sender needs to ensure a secrecy statement is sent and viewed before the email is read. For this reason, many solicitors' firms' disclaimers/confidentiality notices appear before the email is read or the confidential letter is included as an attachment to the email. Telling people something is confidential after they have read it is too late, in law.

Some companies also include statements about viruses - that the recipient is responsible for checking, not the sender and others tell the recipient the reply to the email may be read by others within the organisation.

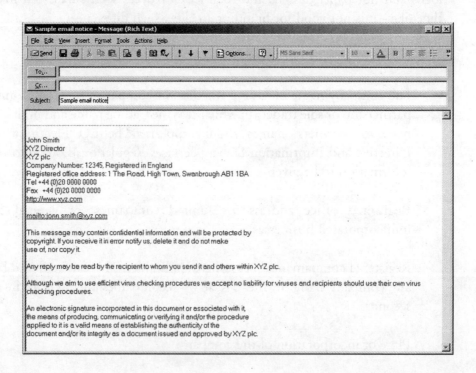

Liability for employers

Emails sent by an employee in the course of their employment will be the responsibility of the employer. The employer is 'vicariously' liable in law for the actions of the employee. If employees make contracts, form cartels, breach copyright or health and safety or libel laws, the employer will be liable, even if the employee was disobeying company rules and regulations. This may seem very unfair, but it is the law. In one House of Lords case, regarding Ready Mixed Concrete, the court even held an employer liable for anti-competitive agreements that employees had entered into, which were in direct breach of company policy, carried out without company directors' knowing and despite the employees having signed statements regularly, saying they had not engaged in these practices.

This means it is crucial to keep a watch on what employees do.

Employers have been obliged to pay out hundreds of thousands of pounds in libel damages because of statements made by employees in emails. Surveillance can help ensure the libellous material is not sent in the first place.

Surveillance legislation

The Regulation of Investigatory Powers Act 2000 and Telecommunications (Lawful Business Practice) (Interception of Communications) Regulations 2000 (Statutory Instrument 2000/2699) contain the latest laws applicable to surveillance of employee emails and telephone calls. The regulations came into force on 24 October 2000.

They allow employers to intercept emails and telephone calls of employees and customers/suppliers, without their consent:

· to establish the existence of facts relevant to the business;

- to ascertain compliance with regulatory or self-regulatory practices or procedures relevant to the business;

- to ascertain or demonstrate standards that are or ought to be achieved by persons using the telecoms system;

- to prevent or detect crime;

- to investigate or detect the unauthorised use of their telecoms systems;

- to ensure the effective operation of the system.

The Regulations also authorise businesses to monitor (but not record), without consent, in the following cases:

- for the purpose of determining whether or not they are communications relevant to the business, for example, checking email accounts to access business communications in staff absence;

- in the case of communications to a confidential anonymous counselling or support helpline, for example, monitoring calls to confidential, welfare helplines in order to protect or support helpline staff.

Staff whose communications may be intercepted without their consent should be told.

The DTI says:

e.g. businesses could place a note in staff contracts or in other readily available literature informing staff that interceptions may take place. The persons who use a system are the people who make direct use of it. Someone who calls from outside, or who receives a call outside, using another system is not a user of the system on which the interception is made.

> **Tip**
>
> The financial liabilities arising from an employee breaching copyright, libelling others, entering into contracts, etc. are much greater than the losses that might arise if the employer breaches the employee's privacy rights.

Privacy laws and surveillance

Where personal data is involved, however, compliance with other laws is necessary. The Information Commissioner published a draft Code of Practice, in part relevant to this area, under the Data Protection Act 1998 and the Human Rights Act 1998, which came into force on 2 October 2000, protecting privacy of personal correspondence. However, an employer with a consistent policy that bans employees' use of employer systems for personal emails and internet access at work need have little to fear from this legislation.

The Information Commissioner was the former Data Protection Commissioner or Registrar. She was renamed in 2001, when the Freedom of Information Act 2000 came into force. In her draft Code she writes:

There is no Data Protection provision that requires an employer to allow employees to use the employer's telephone system, e-mail system or internet access for personal communications.... Monitoring of business communications might also intrude on an employee's privacy or autonomy to the extent that personal data are processed unfairly. For example, employees might well want to impart personal information by telephone or e-mail for business reasons which they only want to be revealed to the intended recipients, such as, personal reasons for asking for a meeting to be postponed. They may also have legitimate concerns about constraints on their autonomy at work. The extent to which these are justified may depend on the nature of the work, but routine monitoring of the content of all communications sent and received at work is in many cases likely to go too far.

The Code is still in draft and the finalised version may differ when issued late in 2001/2002.

Sacking email and internet abusers

The most practical advice readers can be given when they propose to sack an employee for activities engaged upon on the internet or by email is to take legal advice from an employment lawyer. Details of lawyers specialised in this and other fields are in the Chambers and Partners' Directory, which is free on the internet at www.chambersandpartners.com.

The employment contract should be followed to the letter as should any procedures set out in the company's disciplinary procedures. Policies should be consistently and fairly applied. Often, there are good grounds for dismissal, but the manner in which it is done results in an action for unfair dismissal.

If the employer has not prohibited private use of email and indeed has allowed it to go on, then sacking someone may be unfair dismissal. A claim for over £50,000 in damages might be brought and this could be even higher if there is sex discrimination involved in the dismissal.

Examples of sackings for internet abuse

- Orange sacked 40 employees for distributing 'inappropriate material' in September 2000.

- Cable & Wireless sacked six staff in the same year for breach of its policies in this area, too.

Summary

Employers should have a written policy to inform employees of their rights or restrictions in relation to use of the internet and email at work. The policy will not only cover private use of emails and the internet, but also how the employee should conduct him or herself as regards corporate email use. The example employee policy at the end of this chapter shows some of the areas that may be considered. Adding a clause to employment contracts, making it clear that surveillance may occur and that the employee consent to this, is also a useful precaution.

Appendix to Chapter 8

Example Email and Internet Policy for Employees

XYZ Plc.
Email and Internet Policies

1.   Email

1.1   We encourage employees to use email at work. It saves time and expense. However, we do require that you follow the simple rules below. These are part of your staff handbook with which, in turn, you are required to comply under your employment contract. A serious breach of these rules could lead to dismissal. If you are unsure about whether anything you propose to do might breach our email policy, speak to your manager or the company secretary for advice first.

1.2   Although we encourage the use of email, it can be risky. You need to be careful not to introduce viruses on to our system. You need to take proper account of the security advice below. You must make sure you do not send libellous statements in emails as the company could be liable for damages.

1.3   These rules are designed to minimise the legal risks we run when you use email at work and access the internet. They are also designed to tell you what you may and may not do at work in this area. If there is something we have not covered and you do not know what our policy is then ask your manager or the company secretary. Do not assume you know the right answer.

1.4   Technology and the law change all the time and this policy will be updated regularly. It is your responsibility to read the latest version of this document which will be both emailed and sent to you in the internal mail.

Example Email and Internet Policy for Employees (continued)

2. Using the internet at work

2.1 Authorised Internet Users: If you have been provided with a computer with internet access at your desk you may use the internet at work. If there is access through one terminal in your department and you have been told you may use the internet, then again you may do so. If you have not been told or do not know, then ask.

2.2 Not everyone in the company needs access to the internet at work. If you think you do, but have not been given access so far, then contact your manager and make a written request setting out your reasons why you think the access should be allowed.

2.3 You are not allowed to arrange your own internet access on the PC on your desk. All internet access must be officially sanctioned and put in place by our trained IT professionals.

2.4 Personal lap tops: You may not bring your own laptop or palmtop or other computer or other device into work to surf the internet or send emails during working hours unless you have been permitted to do so by your manager. The reason for this is that use of the internet where the company does not deem it necessary can waste time in your day working for the company. Also we cannot monitor the access you make over your own system in the way we can over our own systems. If you bring a mobile telephone into work you may not make outgoing calls except during your rest breaks.

2.5 If you are allowed access to the internet at work then you are expected to use it sensibly and not so that it interferes with efficient working for the company. For example if it would be quicker for you to call a standards body than do a long-winded internet search then make a telephone call instead. You may be called upon to

Example Email and Internet Policy for Employees (continued)

justify the amount of time you have spent on the internet or the sites you have visited so always bear this in mind when surfing the net.

2.6 We encourage those to whom we give internet access to become familiar with the internet and do not currently impose any time limitation on work-related internet use. We trust employees not to abuse the latitude we give them, but if this trust is abused, then we reserve the right to alter the policy in this respect.

2.7 Removing internet access: We can at any time deny internet access to any employee at work without giving any reason, although normally we would provide reasons.

2.8 Registering on web sites: If you want to register as a user of a web site for work purposes this is encouraged. Many such sites are very useful for the company and a large number require a registration. You should ask your manager in advance, however, so we are sure of that to which you may be committing the company and to ensure the registration will not result in our being inundated with junk mail. You should check any boxes to show we do not want our data used for other marketing purposes.

2.9 Licences and contracts: Some sites through which you can access free work-related information and documents will require the company to enter into licence or contract terms. These terms would be checked by our legal department in the normal way. The fact they are electronic does not affect our normal rules in this respect. Print off the terms and send them for approval in advance or email them to the legal department before you agree to them on the company's behalf. In most cases they will be unobjectionable and the free information to which you will then be entitled may save the company money. Always consider, however, whether the information is from a reputable source and is likely to be accurate

Example Email and Internet Policy for Employees (continued)

and kept up to date. Most of the contract terms you will be required to sign up to will exclude liability for accuracy for such free information.

2.10 Downloading files and software: Only download files on to PCs with virus checking software and check how long the download will take. If you are uncertain as to whether the time it will take is reasonable, ask your line manager. In some cases, it will be cheaper for us to order the software or file on disk by telephone rather than spending, for example, two hours downloading a file which may prevent your doing your normal work in the meantime. Check with our IT department before you download software. It may not be compatible with our system or may cause other problems.

2.11 Using other software at work: Our staff handbook does not allow you to bring software into the office from home without the IT department's consent and nothing in this Email and Internet Policy modifies our general policies on such software use.

3. Using the internet for personal purposes

3.1 Where you are given access to the internet at work, you may access the internet, using our systems, during your official lunch and rest breaks, but at no other times, provided no other employee needs use of the PC for work-related purposes, for personal purposes so long as:

- such use is limited to no more than 20 minutes in any day;

- you do not order goods or services, including stocks and shares, without your manager's permission (in many cases this may be granted but we want to know about this in advance);

Example Email and Internet Policy for Employees (continued)

- you do not access any site that will result in charges being levied for such access over and above the cost of the local call in most internet access;

- you do not use the internet to access unlawful material - if by accident you access unlawful material you should send an email to your manager so we know the circumstances (the access may be picked up by our monitoring system); (for these purposes unlawful material is that which breaks English law such as child pornography and also searches within the law but which may expose the company to liability for sexual harassment by other colleagues who may see what you are searching - such as soft pornography);

- you do not enter into any contracts or commitments in the name of or on behalf of the company;

- you do not arrange for any goods ordered after you have obtained your manager's approval to be delivered to our address or order them in the company's name.

3.2   You are not allowed to use the internet at other times for personal purposes, including before working hours begin or after they end. We have security concerns about staff arriving early and leaving late and it is harder for us to monitor your use of the internet at such times. During your working hours you must not surf the internet at all for personal purposes. This is in line with our policy on the use of office telephones and faxes and our restriction on your use of your personal mobile telephone to official breaks only. If you are not sure what a 'personal purpose' is ask your manager. It means something unrelated to your job.

4.   Use of Email

4.1   Where we have given you access to email at work you may send work-related emails.

Example Email and Internet Policy for Employees (continued)

4.2 Staff may not send or receive personal emails at work using the company's computers. Staff using their own lap or palm tops or personal organisers to send private emails shall do so only in official lunch and rest breaks and not use the company name or affiliations in any way.

4.3 Ensure our official corporate information is given on the email, as notified to you. This is set out below but may be varied from time to time. You will be given notice of variations.

> John Smith
> XYZ Director
> XYZ plc
> Company Number: 12345, Registered in England
> Registered office address: 1 The Road, High Town, Swanbrough AB1 1BA
> Tel: +44 (0)20 0000 0000
> Fax: +44 (0)20 0000 0000
> Web site: http://www.xyz.com
> mailto:jonn.smith@xyz.com

'This message may contain confidential information and will be protected by copyright. If you receive it in error notify us, delete it and do not make use of, nor copy it.

Any reply may be read by the recipient to whom you send it and others within XYZ plc.

Although we aim to use efficient virus checking procedures, we accept no liability for viruses and recipients should use their own virus checking procedures.

Example Email and Internet Policy for Employees (continued)

> An electronic signature incorporated in this document or associated with it, the means of producing, communicating or verifying it and/or the procedure applied to it is a valid means of establishing the authenticity of the document and/or its integrity as a document issued and approved by XYZ plc.
>
> When you send emails to employees of our company please note these may be read and copied throughout our company.'

4.4   Read emails carefully several times. It is just as important as with a letter that they are accurate and do not contain typing and spelling errors. They are often the written public face of the company. In many cases, for longer emails, it may be better to prepare the message offline and check it carefully before despatch.

4.5   Libel: The company can be sued for libel if you make inaccurate statements in your emails that disparage or denigrate other people or companies. This could lead to our having to pay hundreds of thousands of pounds in damages and you would lose your job. Therefore read all messages carefully before sending them and if in doubt at all about what you have written check the content with your manager first.

4.6   CCing: Be very careful not to copy emails automatically to all those copied in with the original message to which you are replying. It is easy to do this and can mean a message is seen by someone you do not want to see it. It may mean you disclose confidential company information to the wrong person. Disable the automatic 'ccing back' function on the email and then with each email consider who should be copied with it.

4.7   Statements to avoid include criticising our competitors or their staff, stating there are quality problems with goods or services of suppliers or customers and stating anyone is incompetent.

Example Email and Internet Policy for Employees (continued)

4.8   If you prepare an email and your overall feeling is that you are glad you have 'got it off your chest' it is probably a signal it should not be sent. Do not prepare such emails. It is easy for you or your secretary to send them in error or for them to be seen by someone else. It rarely reflects well on the company, in any event, to criticise others. The quality of our goods and services speak for themselves.

4.9   Do not attach anything to an email that may contain a virus. The company could be liable to the recipient for loss suffered. We have virus checking in place but check with our IT department in cases of doubt. Be very careful about forwarding attachments from third parties, particularly unidentified third parties. These may carry viruses and they may also not have been cleared for copyright issues. You may breach copyright by sending them on to someone else as you are making a further copy. The company could be sued for large damages for breach of copyright.

4.10 Email Monitoring: We routinely monitor your emails and web sites accessed at work to ensure compliance with the law, your employment contract, these conditions and other purposes, in the same way your manager may read your business letters and faxes. If you want to send confidential non-work-related emails, do so on your own equipment in your own time at your own home. Ensure you tell your personal email contacts never to send you any personal emails at work.

5.   Contracts

5.1   You should have been told by the company whether you have authority to enter into contracts on behalf of the company. If you do not know ask your manager. You may be subject to a financial limit above which you may not enter into contracts. Stick to these rules and limits when ordering goods or services or supplying them

Example Email and Internet Policy for Employees (continued)

via email. Most staff are not allowed to make contracts on the company's behalf. However, what follows below will apply to our procurement/buying department and our contracts department.

5.2 The company is happy for contracts to be formed electronically and encourages this to be done. However, it should only be done by those with authority, should accord with our contract management policy in any event and should follow the rules below for electronic contracts:

- Do not order anything without knowing the delivery dates and if they are legally binding; the price; clear description of the goods; full identity of the supplier; payment method and delivery charges if any. Be cautious about ordering high value goods or services with payment in advance.

- Read the terms and conditions and print out a copy for the relevant paper file. We may need to refer to the terms later if a legal dispute arises. Make sure you are happy with them. Check them with our legal department.

- Try to enter contracts on our own terms and conditions of purchase wherever possible, in the usual way. Our lawyers can advise you on how to do this.

  Conversely, when you agree on behalf of the company to supply goods or services, make sure you use our standard terms and conditions of supply.

- The contract terms should be sent before the contract is made, otherwise it may be too late in contract law terms for them to form part of the legal arrangement. This is very important.

- Make sure you have a supplier telephone number, fax and physical address and full company name, otherwise we may have no practical recourse against the supplier if things go wrong.

Example Email and Internet Policy for Employees (continued)

- Ensure you know when a contract is made - when we are legally bound to proceed. Do not pull out or attempt to pull out after that stage without taking legal advice first.

5.3 Where there is a negotiated contract take advice from our company secretary or legal department about whether, in that case, we are happy to send contract drafts by email. In many cases we are, but some deals are particularly secret and other methods must be used. If we are happy with this, then do be careful to check for changes made by the other company. Sometimes a marked up draft does not show all the changes. Also, watch out for disclosure of any comments you make on the draft. Although you may think you have deleted them before sending them to the other company, they may be readable using some word processing software.

5.4 When you reach the final contract signature stage, at present we still require a physical signature on negotiated contracts of this type so ensure a faxed or posted or couriered copy of the contract is signed. The Electronic Communications Act 2000 does provide for judicial recognition of 'electronic signatures' but our company has not yet authorised any employees to purchase such technology. We will notify you if and when we introduce them.

6. Copyright

6.1 Most information available electronically is protected by copyright in the same way as a book, music or a play is. The Copyright, Designs and Patents Act 1988 sets out the rules and you must be careful not to breach copyright. If you do, then the company could have to pay thousands of pounds in damages and you could lose your job.

Example Email and Internet Policy for Employees (continued)

6.2 It is easy to copy electronically but this does not make it any less an offence. The company's policy is to comply with copyright laws. We do not bend the rules in any way. We do not allow the use of pirated or copied computer software. All software must be licensed. We take this very seriously indeed and have regular audits to check the position. We have a separate company policy on use of software at work which also applies. Nothing in this document alters that policy.

6.3 Do not assume that because a document or file is on the internet or our intranet for example that it can be freely copied. There is a difference between information in the 'public domain' (which is certainly then no longer confidential or secret information but is still copyright protected) and information that is not protected by copyright (such as where the author has been dead for more than 70 years under the 1988 Act).

6.4 Copyright and database right law can be complicated. Speak to your manager or the legal department/company secretary if you are unsure about anything.

6.5 Lots of information on the internet says what its copyright conditions are so read those before downloading or copying. For example the Department of Trade and Industry produce useful guidance notes on lots of areas relevant to our business. We would encourage those of you with internet access to download these, but you would not be permitted to reproduce them in a book or other company document without obtaining separate consent.

6.6 Nor must you circulate newspaper cuttings even if just about the company, without speaking to the company secretary first. We do pay for an annual licence from the Newspaper Licensing Agency but you must check first what this covers.

Example Email and Internet Policy for Employees (continued)

6.7 If someone tells you to ignore these rules, even your manager, do not listen to them. Report the matter to our company secretary or a director.

7. Trade Marks, Links and Data Protection

7.1 The company's name is a registered trade mark. If you come across anyone using the same or a similar name, let your manager know. We may need to stop them doing this; but do not send any threatening emails to them about this as that could be an offence under the Trade Marks Act 1994. Our lawyers will handle that side of things.

7.2 You must not register any new domain names or trade marks relating to the company's names or products anywhere in the world, unless the company has authorised it. Nor should you link any of our web pages to any others without checking first with your manager and the company secretary.

7.3 If you see anything on our web site that is not up to date, let your manager know as we need for legal and public relations reasons to keep it accurate and current.

7.4 The company is registered under the Data Protection Act 1998. The 8th data protection principle restricts those countries to which we can send 'personal data' whether by email or any other means. Personal data would be information such as names and addresses or other personal details. Certain data such as about people's race or religion is called 'sensitive personal data' and subject to even stricter rules. You must take legal advice before exporting data. For example even sending a candidate's curriculum vitae from the personnel office in the UK to our associated companies outside the EU could breach the rules if we do not take special measures.

Example Email and Internet Policy for Employees (continued)

8.   General

8.1   The aim of these rules is to be helpful. They are not aimed at putting employees off using the internet or email. We encourage the use of the internet and email. It is a major opportunity for our business.

8.2   If there is anything in the rules that becomes unworkable or which you do not understand, let your manager know and we will do our best to correct or alter the rules. We want them to work and be understood. If you notice another employee not following the code tell them and your manager.

8.3   No matter what we say in these rules or in any other company document your overriding objective must be to obey the law. The company will never ask you to breach the law whatever the circumstances. Contact a director or our external legal advisers if you think you have been asked to do so.

8.4   We sometimes use self- employed contractors or individuals employed by agencies in our company. They will have signed our standard contractor's agreement. They should also be subject to the rules set out in this document, where applicable. If you are working with such contractors show them the rules. The same applies to new members of staff who ought to have been shown a copy.

_____

Signed: Managing Director, the Company

Chapter 9

Other legal issues

Chapter 9

Other legal issues

Summary

· Computer viruses
· Cyber-crimes and hacking
· Litigation issues
· Lawyers and the internet

This chapter considers some remaining legal issues arising from the internet and electronic commerce which have not been covered in other chapters of this book.

Computer viruses

Computer viruses cost companies thousands of pounds. Well-known recent viruses such as the Kournikova and Melissa viruses crippled many companies for days. They spread quickly around the world and often the perpetrator is not caught.

Companies should have virus checking software in place, and firewalls. Many companies will update such software at least weekly. It is sensible to include a statement about viruses on emails such as that mentioned on Chapter 8. The recipient of the email is given responsibility for the virus checking.

If an agreement is in place for the supply of data or computer software, frequently it will contain a term or condition about viruses. Most companies commissioning computer software will have a written contract with the supplier of the software and will include a term that the supplier warrants that the material produced does not contain viruses. That is a case where a provider is being paid to supply software. Where an email is sent, the situation is different. There may well be no contract between the parties and it is not usually the case that the sender is liable for the damages caused to the recipient from the virus.

Cyber-crimes and hacking

Computer Misuse Act 1990

The Computer Misuse Act 1990 makes it a criminal offence to gain unauthorised access to computer systems and, separately, a further offence, once having gained such access, to modify material. There are few prosecutions, although a special department of police forces around the country handles this area - the computer crimes unit. Many employers do not want to draw public attention to problems with their own security so offences are covered up or not much reported. Even when prosecutions are brought before local courts, the penalties are often weak.

Other countries have similar hacking legislation, so a hacker who has been hacking in many nations may find him or herself prosecuted in a number of different locations. The US Department of Justice is active in the computer crime area and has a cyber-crime web site at www.cybercrime.gov.

Copyright, Designs and Patents Act 1988

The same is the case with criminal offences under the Copyright, Designs and Patents Act 1988. Sentences can be light. Some computer software owners will seek to have a criminal prosecution brought against a computer software pirate or counterfeiter as a threat of a jail sentence can be more of a deterrent to some individuals than a large damages claim or seizure of the infringing programs.

FAST and BSA

Bodies such as the Federation Against Software Theft (FAST) (www.fast.org.uk) and Business Software Alliance (BSA) (www.bsa.org/uk) will obtain court orders on behalf of their members to seize infringing products. They also help companies ensure that all software used within a business is properly licensed and they run a telephone line for infringements to be reported, with rewards of thousands of pounds paid to those tipping off the organisation about infringement of copyright where this leads to a successful prosecution.

Pirated software

Businesses buying software online need to ensure it is not pirated. The BSA estimates that more than 90 per cent of the software sold on auction sites is pirated The BSA runs an Online Investigative Unit, which recently looked at counterfeit software on Internet auction sites in the US and Europe. Its investigation, called 'Operation Bidder Beware', found sales of pirated or counterfeit software from vendors in the UK, Germany and the US. Each of the 13 defendants caught in the US faces damages of up to $150,000 per work infringed.

Litigation issues

Where use of the internet or email results in legal action in any of the areas covered by this book, whether it be liability arising from an offensive email, breach of copyright, goods supplied online proving defective, or whatever, it is sensible to seek legal advice at an early stage. Even if that advice is only a 20-minute telephone call of advice from a solicitor, expensive mistakes can be avoided by early action.

If a court claim (formerly called a 'writ') arrives, do not delay. There will be time limits, and failure to respond in time can lead to judgment in default of defence being obtained against the recipient.

Lawyers and the internet

Following the advice in this book may help reduce the risk of legal disputes arising. Where those operating electronically are aware of relevant legislation, there is less likely to be a need to instruct solicitors. However, it is generally sensible to have a computer lawyer cast their eyes over any proposed terms and conditions before they are put in use on a web site. Laws change, so terms may need to be updated from time to time and the issues which arise in practice when selling or advertising online can have an impact on what modifications should be made to terms on a web site, on a regular basis.

If a claim is made against a company or a company wishes to send a solicitor's letter or issue court proceedings, then it is sensible to instruct a lawyer to advise. The following points should be considered:

· Never litigate as a matter of principle or in anger; always consider the risks and rewards carefully.

· Assume that legal costs will be double what is estimated, to be on the safe side.

· Check if there is legal expenses insurance in place or if a policy can be purchased to cover the costs.

· If the claim relates to goods supplied or work done, check whether it should be put in the hands of any insurers immediately. Delay can invalidate professional indemnity and product liability insurance policies.

· If it is a simple case of recovery of money, etc., it may be possible to convince a solicitor to take it on on a no-win-no-fee ('conditional fee') basis, although if the case succeeds, the lawyer is allowed to charge double the usual charges, and if it is lost, the other side's costs will still have to be paid or an insurance policy paid for to cover such costs.

- Ask the lawyers for their hourly rate or how they will charge, and ask for an estimate in writing. Agree a cap over which fees will not be incurred without consent in writing from the client. Specialist lawyers tend to have an hourly rate they charge depending on the seniority of the lawyer involved. Partners in specialist London firms are likely to charge from about £275 - £400 an hour (2001 rates), but out of London in more general practices hourly rates of £110 - £200 are more the norm. If the matter goes to court, a barrister may need to be retained and paid for, as well. Ask for an estimate of their charges in writing, too. In litigation, experts will often need to be paid for, too - again have agreed estimates of their charges.

- Remember that complex computer/IT disputes and claims about trade marks and copyright are very expensive. Few such disputes result in legal costs of under £100,000 if the matter goes to trial and this is the main issue - more than 90 per cent of cases settle before then. One solicitor's letter may cost under £200 and that may be the end of the matter, or a complex trial costing £500,000 may be involved. Always consider what will be gained if a matter is fought compared with the costs if it is lost.

Conclusion

Many areas of English law apply to those doing business online or using email in the course of their business. None of these laws is sufficiently onerous to deter any business from taking the opportunity to trade in this way and in many cases, the laws provide valuable and useful protection for both businesses and consumers alike.

Index

E

Electronic Communications Act 2000 104, 107–8

email 3, 51, 123
  accuracy in 137
  contracts by 103–4, 107
  electronic signatures 104, 107–8, 137
  employees
        policies 131, 135–8
        surveillance on 138
  freedom of communication 52
  preference schemes 56
  status 125
  unsolicited 52
        opting-in schemes 53–4
        opting-out schemes 53, 56

employees 123
  access rights for 124
  conduct 130
  copyright ownership 20
  dismissals 129–30
  employers' liabilities 127
  policies 10
        on access rights 130–3
        on conduct 132
        on confidentiality 137
        on contracts 138–40
        on copyright 138, 140–2
        coverage 143
        on criticism 137–8
        on downloading 134
        on electronic signatures 137
        on email 131, 135–8
        on libel 137
        on links 142
        on own hardware 132
        on personal data 142
        on personal use 134–5
        on software 134
        on terms and conditions 133–4, 139
        on trade marks 142
        on viruses 138
  surveillance of 106, 124, 127–8
        emails 138

exports, of data, clauses 55–6, 57
  on appropriate uses 66, 68
  on automated decisions 68
  coverage 64–5
  definitions 58
  on direct marketing 67–8
  disclosure 62
  on dispute negotiations 61–2
  on exporters 59
  on further exports 66–7, 69
  immutability 63
  on importers 59–61
  on personal data 67
  safeguards 62, 65–9
  on subjects' rights 58, 61, 66–7, 68–9
  transfers 58

F

FAST (Federation Against Software Threat) 149
faxes, unsolicited 56

More books available from Law Pack...

How to Make Money Online

Forget the high-profile dot com failures - there are businesses out there making money online. This guide includes what will and won't sell, how to avoid e-business mistakes, how to give website visitors the confidence to buy online, getting payments, security software and systems, digital certificates and e-signatures, selling advertising space, supplying content, and much more!

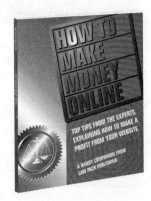

Code B604	ISBN 1 902646 76 2	PB	
250 x 199mm	160pp	£9.99	Jan 2002

Online Marketing Strategies

What are your goals for your website? Is your website marketing you, or are you marketing it? And how will your website relate to your business's overall marketing strategy? This book provides guidance on building marketing into your website, on monitoring, evaluating and improving your internet or extranet site and on coordinating online and offline marketing strategies.

Code B602	ISBN 1 902646 75 4	PB	
250 x 199mm	160pp	£9.99	Oct 2001

Secrets of Successful Web Sites

Some web sites get it right, many get it wrong. This guide divulges what makes a successful site. It covers identifying the audience and their needs, choosing the right content and design, writing for your web site, choosing the right technology and internet service provider, DIY versus professional web design and knowing how to deal with specialist web designers.

Code B601	ISBN 1 902646 74 6	PB	
250 x 199mm	160pp	£9.99	Nov 2001

To order, visit www.lawpack.co.uk or call 020 7394 4040

More books available from Law Pack...

Legal Advice Handbook

Where do you go for legal advice? As the sources of both free and paid-for legal advice become more diverse and specific areas of law demand greater specialisation from the advice givers, the need for a consumer guide to this expanding, unmapped network has never been greater. Solicitor Tessa Shepperson has gathered together extensive research data and produced an invaluable handbook.

Code B427	ISBN 1 902646 71 1	PB	
A5	130pp	£7.99	October 2001

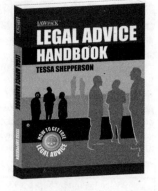

Creativity at Work

Encouraging staff to become more creative has proved to boost morale and raise the bottom line. Creativity can turn around a business. This book includes exercises in developing your thinking skills, 'greenhousing' and other thinking tools, putting creativity into the culture of an organisation, case studies across industry and an action plan for turning a business into a creative powerhouse.

Code B428	ISBN 1 902646 78 9	PB	
250 x 199mm	160pp	£9.99	Dec 2001

Tax Answers at a Glance

With the emphasis on self-assessment, we all need to have a hold of the panoply of taxes now levied by government. Compiled by tax experts and presented in question-and- answer format, this handy guide provides a useful summary of income tax, VAT, capital gains, inheritance, pensions, self-employment, partnerships, land and property, trusts and estates, corporation tax, stamp duty and more.

Code B425	ISBN 1 902646 62 2	PB	
A5	130pp	£7.99	April 2001

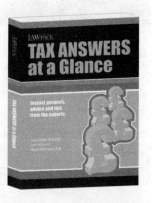

To order, visit www.lawpack.co.uk or call 020 7394 4040

More books available from Law Pack...

Look out for the Professor! Made Easy Guides are practical, self-help business reference books which take you step by step through the subject in question.

- Legal and business titles
- Experts' advice
- 'How to' information and instructions
- Save professional fees!

Business Letters I & II

Business Letters I and *Business Letters II* are complementary Made Easy Guides, each providing an invaluable source of more than 100 ready-drafted letters for a range of business situations. Each letter has a useful commentary which helps you choose the right turn of phrase. The *Business Letters Made Easy* Guides take the headache and time-wasting out of letter writing, and provide you with letters that get results.

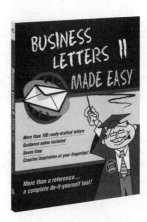

Code B504	ISBN 1 902646 38 X	PB
250 x 199mm	142pp	£9.99	1st edition

Code B505	ISBN 1 902646 39 8	PB
250 x 199mm	152pp	£9.99	1st edition

Negotiating Tactics

What business can expect success without being able to negotiate good deals? In today's competitive world, you need to know about the tactics and techniques which professional negotiators use to win. *Negotiating Tactics Made Easy* pools the expertise of 12 experienced negotiators and is packed with advice and tips on handling almost any situation. Be prepared for the ploys and techniques you are bound to come up against!

Code B507	ISBN 1 902646 45 2	PB
250 x 199mm	234pp	£9.99	1st edition

To order, visit www.lawpack.co.uk or call 020 7394 4040

More books available from Law Pack...

Limited Company Formation

Incorporation as a limited liability company is the preferred structure for thousands of successful businesses. *Limited Company Formation Made Easy* Guide explains why, and shows you how to set up your own limited liability company easily and inexpensively. It provides detailed but easy to follow instructions, background information, completed examples of Companies House forms and drafts of other necessary documents.

Code B503	ISBN 1 902646 43 6	PB	
250 x 199mm	112pp	£9.99	1st edition

Profitable Mail-Order

Mail-order business is big business, and it's growing year by year. Setting up and running your own mail-order business can be fun as well as profitable. This *Made Easy* Guide shows you how to do it, explaining the vital importance of product profile, building valuable mailing lists, effective advertising and a whole lot more. It divulges the mail-order secrets that ensure success!

Code B510	ISBN 1 902646 46 0	PB	
250 x 199mm	206pp	£9.99	1st edition

Running Your Own Business

You have a business idea that you want to put into action, but you also want advice on the realities of setting up and running a business: this *Made Easy* Guide is for you. It takes you through the business-creation process, from assessing your aptitude and ideas, to funding and business plans.

Code B511	ISBN 1 902646 47 9	PB	
250 x 199mm	140pp	£9.99	1st edition